INVESTING IN ETERNITY

UNDERSTANDING GOD'S HEART FOR HIS CHURCH

A 28-DAY JOURNEY DEVOTIONAL

GARY J. MORITZ

100x
PRESS

Copyright © 2025 by Gary J. Moritz, Jana G. Moritz

Publisher: The Church Vitality Network - 100x Press

Cover and Layout Design: Gary J. Moritz

Author Photo: Jaden Rivers, Jenesis Photography

ISBN: 979-8-9868325-1-7

All rights reserved.

No part of this book may be reproduced in any form or by any electronic or mechanical means, including information storage and retrieval systems, without written permission from the author, except for the use of brief quotations in a book review.

Scripture taken from the New King James Version®. Copyright © 1982 by Thomas Nelson. Used by permission. All rights reserved.

This book is dedicated with heartfelt gratitude to my Pastor, Steve Reynolds, whose teachings have deeply inspired me to understand the true Spirit of sacrificial giving for the Kingdom through the local church. His unwavering dedication as a shepherd, leader, and preacher of God's Word to the congregation of Capital Baptist Church has been a tremendous blessing to my family.

"Do not lay up for yourselves treasures on earth, where moth and rust destroy and where thieves break in and steal; but lay up for yourselves treasures in heaven, where neither moth nor rust destroys and where thieves do not break in and steal. For where your treasure is, there your heart will be also".

JESUS

CONTENTS

BEFORE WE BEGIN: A WORD TO THE SKEPTICAL

Maybe you picked up this book because someone gave it to you. Perhaps you're curious about what the Bible says about money and the church. Or maybe you're flat-out skeptical about churches asking for money.

Here's what I want you to know: **You're not alone.**

Jesus himself had strong words for religious leaders who took advantage of people financially. He called them "thieves" and flipped tables when they turned God's house into a marketplace. So if you're skeptical about church and money, you're actually in good company with Jesus.

But here's what else Jesus said: "Where your treasure is, there your heart will be also" (Matthew 6:21). He wasn't trying to get your money. He was trying to protect your heart from idolatry.

This 28-day journey isn't about convincing you to give more money to a church. It's about discovering what Jesus taught about investment, generosity, and building a life that matters. Along the way, you might discover that the local church, when it's functioning the way God designed, is the most significant investment opportunity on the planet.

Charles Spurgeon, the great preacher, understood the connection between faith and finances. He once observed: *"A man's treatment of money is the most decisive test of his character—how he makes it and how he spends it."* Your money reveals whether your faith is genuine or merely cultural Christianity.

A WORD ABOUT GOD'S PROMISES AND PROSPERITY

Before we begin this journey together, I want to address something crucial: **This devotional is not about prosperity theology.**

You will not find promises here that faithful giving guarantees financial wealth, perfect health, or a trouble-free life. That's not the Gospel Jesus preached, and it's not the experience of faithful believers throughout history.

WHAT THIS BOOK IS ABOUT:

This is about **trusting God's character**, not manipulating God's blessings. It's about **faithful stewardship** leading to spiritual transformation, not financial accumulation. It's about **investing in God's kingdom** because we love Him, not because we expect material returns.

The Truth About God's Provision:

God absolutely promises to provide for His children. However, His provision looks different than our culture's definition of success. Sometimes God's provision means:

- **Contentment with little** - "I have learned to be content whatever the circumstances" (Philippians 4:11)
- **Strength in suffering** - "My grace is sufficient for you, for my power is made perfect in weakness" (2 Corinthians 12:9)
- **Daily bread, not abundance** - "Give us today our daily bread" (Matthew 6:11)
- **Eternal treasure over temporal wealth** - "Do not store up for yourselves treasures on earth ... but store up for yourselves treasures in heaven" (Matthew 6:19-20)

What About Financial Hardship?

Some of the most faithful stewards in Scripture and history faced significant financial challenges:

- **Paul** worked as a tentmaker while spreading the Gospel and often lacked basic necessities (2 Corinthians 11:27)
- **The Macedonian churches** gave generously "out of the most severe trial" and "extreme poverty" (2 Corinthians 8:2)
- **Jesus himself** had "nowhere to lay his head" (Matthew 8:20)

The Real Promise:

God's promise isn't that generous Christians will be wealthy. God's promise is that generous Christians will be:

- **Spiritually satisfied** - "Whoever drinks the water I give them will never thirst" (John 4:14)
- **Eternally secure** - "In my Father's house are many rooms" (John 14:2)
- **Purposefully used** - "We are God's handiwork, created in Christ Jesus to do good works" (Ephesians 2:10)
- **Divinely provided for** - "My God will meet all your needs according to the riches of his glory in Christ Jesus" (Philippians 4:19)

A Personal Note:
I've seen faithful people lose jobs, face medical bills, and experience financial stress. I've also seen God provide in unexpected ways, sometimes through miraculous provision, sometimes through the kindness of others, and sometimes through supernatural peace during financial pressure.

This devotional will challenge you to trust God with your finances, but it won't promise that trust will make you rich. Instead, it will show you how biblical stewardship can make you **rich toward God** (Luke 12:21), which is infinitely more valuable than earthly wealth.

Our Foundation Scripture:

"But godliness with contentment is great gain. For we brought nothing into the world, and we can take nothing out of it. But if we have food and clothing, we will be content with that. Those who want to get rich fall into temptation and a trap and into many foolish and harmful desires that plunge people into ruin and destruction. For the love of money is a root of all kinds of evil." - 1 Timothy 6:6-10

Supporting Scriptures:

"Keep your lives free from the love of money and be content with what you have" - Hebrews 13:5

"Look at the birds of the air; they do not sow or reap... yet your heavenly Father feeds them" Matthew 6:26

"I know what it is to be in need, and I know what it is to have plenty... I can do all this through him who gives me strength" Philippians 4:12-13

THE MOST IMPORTANT INVESTMENT: YOUR SOUL

Before we talk about investing your money, we need to talk about investing your soul.

You might be reading this book to learn about finances, but there's something infinitely more important than your money: your relationship with God.

The Problem We All Face

The Bible says, "All have sinned and fall short of the glory of God" (Romans 3:23). That includes you. That includes me. We've all done things that displease God - we've lied, been selfish, ignored God, and put ourselves first.

The consequence of our sin is serious: "The wages of sin is death" (Romans 6:23). Not just physical death, but eternal separation from God. We deserve God's judgment, not His blessing.

God's Solution

But here's the incredible news: "God demonstrates His own love toward us, in that while we were still sinners, Christ died for us" (Romans 5:8).

Jesus Christ, God's perfect Son, came to earth and lived a sinless life. He died on the cross to pay the penalty for your sins and mine. Three days later, He rose from the dead, proving He had conquered sin and death.

Your Choice

Salvation isn't about being good enough or giving enough money to the church. It's about trusting in what Jesus has already done for you.

"If you confess with your mouth the Lord Jesus and believe in your heart that God has raised Him from the dead, you will be saved" (Romans 10:9).

How to Receive Christ

If you've never trusted Jesus Christ as your Savior, you can do so right now. It's as simple as talking to God in prayer:

"God, I know I'm a sinner and I deserve Your judgment. I believe Jesus Christ died on the cross for my sins and rose from the dead. I'm trusting in Jesus alone to save me. Please forgive my sins and give me eternal life. I want to follow You from now on. Amen."

What Happens Next?

If you prayed that prayer sincerely, congratulations! You've made the most important investment of your life. You now have:

- **Forgiveness** - Your sins are completely forgiven (1 John 1:9)
- **Eternal life** - You'll spend forever with God (John 3:16)
- **A new identity** - You're now God's child (John 1:12)
- **Purpose** - God has plans for your life (Ephesians 2:10)

Now You're Ready

Now that you understand God's incredible investment in you through Jesus Christ, you're ready to learn about investing in His kingdom. Everything in this book flows from the Gospel - because when you understand what God has given you, generous living becomes a natural response.

If you prayed to receive Christ today, please tell someone about your decision. Find a Bible-believing church where you can grow in your new faith. And remember: your most significant investment wasn't your money, it was your soul.

If you're already a Christian, let this reminder of the Gospel fuel your generosity. When you remember what Christ has done for you, giving becomes not a burden but a joy.

Visit: www.Cityunited.church/Story

HOW TO USE THIS DEVOTIONAL

You're about to embark on a journey that could change everything about how you view money, generosity, and God's heart for your financial life.

Here's what you need to know:

Start wherever you are. Maybe you're completely skeptical about churches and money. Maybe you've been hurt by religious organizations asking for donations. Perhaps you're a mature believer seeking to deepen your faith. This journey meets you where you are and takes you where God wants you to be.

Take it one day at a time. Each daily reading takes about 10-15 minutes. Read the Scripture passage first, then work through the devotional content. Don't rush ahead - let each day's truth settle in your heart before moving on.

Expect to be challenged. This isn't a devotional that will make you comfortable with the status quo. You'll discover that Jesus talked about money more than heaven and hell combined, and He had strong opinions about how His followers should handle their resources.

Get ready for stories that stick. You'll meet heroes like John Newton (the former slave trader who wrote "Amazing Grace"), Charles Spurgeon (the prince of preachers), and William Carey (the father of modern missions). Their examples will inspire you and show you what's possible when someone decides to invest in forever instead of just today.

Plan to take action. Knowledge without action is worthless. Each week builds toward practical commitments that will transform not just your giving, but your entire relationship with money.

Find your community. This journey is better with others. Consider going through it with your family, small group, or accountability partner. The principles you'll learn work best when lived out in community.

Trust the process. Some days will challenge your assumptions. Some will comfort your fears. Some will convict your heart. All are designed to align your financial life with God's heart and purposes.

What you'll discover:

- Week 1: God's foundational principles for handling money

- Week 2: How biblical stewardship transforms your entire life

- Week 3: Why the local church deserves your investment

- Week 4: How your money choices impact eternity

By day 28, you'll understand why generous, faithful stewardship isn't about God needing your money. It's about your heart needing to give.

CHAPTER 1

WEEK ONE: GOD'S PRINCIPLES OF INVESTMENT

> ***Memory Verse:*** *"Honor the Lord with your possessions, and with the firstfruits of all your increase; so your barns will be filled with plenty, and your vats will overflow with new wine." - Proverbs 3:9-10*

DAY 1: THE PRINCIPLE OF SUBMISSION

Today's Focus: Surrendering to God's Financial Plan

Scripture Reading: James 4:6-10

Let me ask you something: What if I told you there was an investment strategy that had never failed in over 2,000 years? What if I showed you a financial plan designed by someone who owns everything on earth and promises to take care of everyone who follows His system?

You'd probably want to know more.

That's exactly what we're talking about when we discuss biblical investment. But here's the catch - it starts with something our culture hates: **Submission.**

Why Submission Feels Wrong

I get it. The word "submission" makes us uncomfortable. We live in a culture that says, "You do you," and "Follow your heart," and "Never let anyone tell you what to do with your money."

But here's what Jesus said: "If anyone desires to come after Me, let him deny himself, and take up his cross, and follow Me" (Matthew 16:24).

Jesus wasn't asking for your money first. He was asking for your heart. Because He knew something we often forget: **your money follows your heart, not the other way around**.

The Three Steps of Financial Submission

Romans 12:1-2 gives us a roadmap:

1. Submit your body (Romans 12:1) - This means your physical presence matters to God. Showing up to learn about His way of handling money is the first step.

2. Separate from worldly patterns (Romans 12:2) - Don't let culture dictate your giving. The world says "get all you can." God says "give all you can."

3. Seek God's Word (Romans 12:2) - Let Scripture guide your investment decisions, not social media or your broke friends.

What This Looks Like in Real Life

Sarah was drowning in debt when she first heard about biblical stewardship. "I thought God was trying to take more money from me," she told me. "But when I submitted my finances to Him in prayer, He showed me how to get out of debt AND give generously. It was the opposite of what I expected." That's how God works.

> **When you submit your finances to Him, you don't lose control - you gain an advisor who knows the future.**

The Spurgeon Test

Charles Spurgeon used to tell his congregation: "When you give to God's work, you are not giving to get, but giving because you've already gotten everything in Christ."

Here's your challenge: Before you make any financial decision this week - buying coffee, paying bills, whatever - pause and ask, "God, what would submission look like in this moment?"

You might be surprised by what happens.

Prayer for Today: *God, I'm willing to explore what it means to submit my finances to You. Could you please show me what that looks like? Help me trust that your plan for my money is better than my plan. And help me see that submission isn't about you taking from me, but about you giving to me. Amen.*

DAY 2: THE PRINCIPLE OF SERVANTHOOD

TODAY'S FOCUS: **Understanding Your Role as God's Money Manager**

Scripture Reading: Romans 6:16-22

Here's a question that might blow your mind: What if you don't actually own anything?

I know, I know. You worked for that paycheck. You paid for that car. You bought that house. But what if I told you that, from God's perspective, you're not an owner - you're a manager?

The Ultimate Career Change

Before you knew Jesus, you were working for the wrong boss. Romans 6:20 says you were "slaves of sin." And let me tell you, sin is a terrible employer. The pay is death (Romans 6:23), there are no benefits, and the retirement plan is hell.

But when Jesus saved you, something incredible happened. You got the ultimate career change.

> “ **You went from being a slave to sin to being a servant of God.**

What Does God Pay?

Here's where it gets interesting. God doesn't just give you a paycheck - He gives you a purpose. Your paycheck is not the endgame. How you invest in the Kingdom is. It's helpful to keep track of where your money is going, and even more meaningful to understand where God's blessings are being directed.

When you serve God with your money, three things happen:

1. **You get perspective** - You start seeing your money as a tool, not a trophy.
2. **You get peace** - You stop worrying about money because you know your Boss has unlimited resources.
3. **You get purpose** - Every dollar becomes part of something bigger than yourself.

Jesus said it best: "Whoever wants to become great among you must be your servant" (Mark 10:43).

Think about the best managers you know. They don't hoard company resources for their benefit. They utilize these resources to achieve the company's mission. That's exactly what God is asking you to do with "your" money.

A Different Kind of Rich

Emma was a junior in college working part-time at a campus coffee shop. "I was making $8.50 an hour and barely had enough for ramen noodles," she said. "When I heard about tithing, I thought it was impossible."

But Emma decided to trust God with her tiny income. She started giving $2 from every $20 paycheck. "It sounds ridiculous, but those two dollars taught me that God owns everything, including my future career. When I graduated, I had learned to see myself as God's money manager before I even had real money to manage."

Now Emma works in marketing and gives 15% of her income. "Starting small in college built my faith muscle. I learned stewardship when the stakes were low, so I could handle it when my income grew."

William Carey, the father of modern missions, understood the spiritual foundation of stewardship. He said: "Prayer—secret, fervent, believing prayer—lies at the root of all personal godliness." That's the servanthood mindset. Before you manage God's money, you must commune with God's heart. You're not just handling finances - you're stewarding miracles that begin in prayer.

The Reality Check

Here's the truth: You were never really the owner anyway. Everything you have comes from God, will return to God, and can be taken by God at any moment. The question is: Will you fight this reality or embrace it?

When you embrace it, something beautiful happens. You stop being anxious about money and start being excited about what God can do through you.

Prayer for Today: *God, help me see myself as your money manager, not money's owner. Show me how to use the resources you've given me to serve your purposes. Help me find joy in being your servant instead of anxiety in being a slave to money. Make me a good steward of everything You've entrusted to me. Amen.*

DAY 3: THE PRINCIPLE OF SOWING AND REAPING

TODAY'S FOCUS: **Investing with Eternal Perspective**

Scripture Reading: Galatians 6:7-10

Let's talk about farming for a minute. I know many of us couldn't grow a tomato if our lives depended on it, but stick with me here.

Every farmer understands a simple truth: You reap what you sow. Plant corn, get corn. Plant weeds, get weeds. Plant nothing, get nothing.

Jesus often used farming analogies because He knew we needed to understand this principle. But He wasn't just talking about crops. He was talking about money.

The Spiritual Laws of Agriculture

The apostle Paul said, "*But this I say: He who sows sparingly will also reap sparingly, and he who sows bountifully will also reap bountifully.*" (2 Corinthians 9:6) That's not prosperity gospel. That's agricultural gospel.

Here are the laws every farmer (and every investor) needs to understand:

1. You can't harvest what you don't plant - If you never give, you'll never experience the joy of generous living.

2. You reap more than you sow - One seed produces a plant with hundreds of seeds. God multiplies what you give.

3. You reap after you sow - There's always a delay between planting and harvesting. Don't give up too soon.

4. You reap in a different season than you sow - You plant in spring, harvest in fall. Your giving today may not pay off until heaven.

The Best Investment Strategy on Earth

George Whitefield, the great revivalist, once said: "We are immortal until our work on earth is done." The same is true of your money. When you invest it in God's kingdom, it becomes immortal too.

Think about it: the stock market crashes. Real estate bubbles burst. Even gold loses value. But Jesus said, "Heaven and earth will pass away, but My words will by no means pass away" (Matthew 24:35).

When you invest in God's work, you're putting your money in the only market that's guaranteed never to crash.

But What About My Bills?

I hear you. You're thinking, "That's nice and all, but I've got rent to pay and kids to feed." Jesus addressed this exact concern: "But seek first the kingdom of God and His righteousness, and all these things shall be added to you" (Matthew 6:33).

Notice the order: God first, bills second. Not because God doesn't care about your bills, but because He wants to be your provider, not just your emergency fund.

God's "harvest" in your life may be spiritual growth, deeper faith, or eternal rewards rather than financial increase. Trust His wisdom in how He chooses to bless your faithfulness.

The Compound Interest of Generosity

Lisa started giving $20 a week to her church when she was barely making ends meet. "I thought I was crazy," she said. "But over the next year, I got a promotion, found a cheaper apartment, and my car stopped breaking down. I can't prove it was because I started giving, but I can't prove it wasn't either."

Jonathan Edwards said it this way: "Resolution One: I will live for God. Resolution Two: If no one else does, I will."

The Bottom Line

You're going to invest your money somewhere, but it can not be your master or your obsession. The question is: Where will it produce the greatest return?

Jesus gave us the answer: "No one can serve two masters; for either he will hate the one and love the other, or else he will be loyal to the one and despise the other. You cannot serve God and mammon." (Matthew 6:24).

Prayer for Today: *God, help me understand the principle of sowing and reaping. Give me faith to plant seeds in Your kingdom, even when I can't see the harvest yet. Please show me how to invest in eternity while being responsible with my earthly obligations. Help me trust Your timing and Your provision. Amen.*

DAY 4: THE PRINCIPLE OF SACRIFICE

TODAY'S FOCUS: **Giving That Costs You Something**

Scripture Reading: Mark 12:41-44

Here's a story that will mess with everything you think you know about giving:

Jesus was sitting near the temple, watching people give their offerings. The wealthy individuals were investing large sums, likely to ensure that everyone could see their generosity. Then a poor widow came and put in two small coins, worth about a penny.

Jesus called His disciples over and said something shocking: "This poor widow has put in more than all the others. They gave out of their wealth; but she, out of her poverty, put in everything she had to live on" (Mark 12:43-44).

Wait, What?

How can two pennies be more than thousands of dollars? Because Jesus doesn't judge our giving by the amount. He judges it by the sacrifice.

The rich gave what was convenient. The widow gave what was costly.

The rich gave their leftovers. The widow gave her lunch money.

The rich gave from their abundance. The widow gave from her heart.

The Math of Sacrifice

Here's how God's math works:

Sacrifice = Gift ÷ Capacity

If you make $100,000 a year and give $100, that's 0.1% - not much sacrifice.

If you make $20,000 a year and give $1000, that's 5% - a more significant sacrifice.

If you make $15,000 a year and give $1,500, that's 10% - a significant sacrifice.

God doesn't need your money. He owns everything. But He wants your heart. And your heart is revealed by what costs you something.

The Spurgeon Standard

Charles Spurgeon understood the refining power of difficulty. He once observed: "Trials teach us what we are; they dig up the soil, and let us see what we are made of." Spurgeon knew that sacrificial giving reveals true character.

Spurgeon practiced what he preached. Despite being one of the most famous preachers of his time, he gave away most of his income and died with almost nothing in the bank. But he invested millions in eternity.

But I'm Living Paycheck to Paycheck

I get it. You're thinking, "Easy for him to say. He doesn't know my situation."

But here's what Jesus said to people in much worse financial situations than you: "Give, and it will be given to you" (Luke 6:38).

Notice, Jesus didn't say, "Give when you can afford it." He said, "Give, and then I'll make sure you can afford it."

The Widow's Secret

Want to know why the widow gave everything? Because she understood something the rich people didn't: God is more reliable than money.

The rich people trusted in their wealth. The widow trusted in her God.

The rich people played it safe. The widow took a leap of faith.

The rich people gave to be seen. The widow gave to see God work.

The widow's sacrificial giving pleased Jesus because it revealed her heart, not because it guaranteed her financial breakthrough. Sometimes faithful sacrifice leads to continued financial struggle, but always to spiritual blessing.

John Bunyan, who wrote "Pilgrim's Progress" while in prison for preaching, said: "You have not lived today until you have done something for someone who can never repay you."

Your Move

Here's your challenge: Ask God to show you what sacrificial giving looks like for you. It might be $5. It might be $50. It might be $500. The amount doesn't matter. The sacrifice does.

And here's a promise from Jesus: "Whoever loses their life for me will find it" (Matthew 16:25). The same is true of your money.

Prayer for Today: *Jesus, help me understand the difference between convenient giving and sacrificial giving. Please show me what it means to give in a way that costs me something. Give me the faith to trust You with my finances, just as the widow trusted You with her last two coins. Please help me find joy in sacrifice. Amen.*

DAY 5: THE PRINCIPLE OF STEADFASTNESS

TODAY'S FOCUS: **Consistent, Faithful Investment**

Scripture Reading: 1 Corinthians 15:58

Let me tell you about two gardeners.

Gardener #1 gets excited about growing tomatoes. He buys the best seeds, the finest soil, and top-of-the-line tools. He plants with enthusiasm, waters religiously for two weeks, and then ... life happens. He gets busy, forgets to water, and by the end of summer, his garden is dead.

Gardener #2 plants the same seeds in average soil with basic tools. But every day, rain or shine, motivated or not, busy or free, he shows up. He waters, weeds, and tends his garden. By the end of summer, he's eating fresh tomatoes.

The difference? Steadfastness.

Why Consistency Beats Intensity

John Newton (yes, the "Amazing Grace" guy) said: "We serve a God who makes rough places smooth, and crooked things straight, but He does it in His time and in His way."

Most people approach giving like Gardener #1. They get emotionally moved by a sermon or a missions video and make a significant one-time gift. Then life happens, emotions fade, and their giving stops.

But Jesus said: "He who is faithful in what is least is faithful also in much" (Luke 16:10).

God is more impressed by the person who gives $25 every month than the person who gives $500 once and never gives again.

The Doctrine of Steadfastness

Paul tells us to study God's Word consistently (2 Timothy 2:15). The same principle applies to giving. You need to research what God says about money and use it steadily, not sporadically.

Here's what steady givers understand that emotional givers don't:

1. Giving is worship, not a reaction - You don't give because you feel like it. You give because God is worthy.

2. Faithfulness builds trust - The more consistently you give, the more you trust God with your finances.

3. Consistency creates margin - When you give regularly, you budget for it. When you give emotionally, you often give money you don't have.

The Duty of Steadfastness

Here's what might surprise you: The Bible presents giving as a duty, not just an opportunity.

William Carey, the missionary, understood what matters most. He said, "I am not afraid of failure; I am afraid of succeeding at things that don't matter." Carey feared wasting his life on temporal pursuits while neglecting eternal investments.

That's the heart of steadfastness. It's not about having tremendous faith every day. It's about consistently investing in what matters to God, whether you feel like it or not.

The Devotion of Steadfastness

But steadfastness isn't just gritting your teeth and powering through. It's finding your strength in Christ (Philippians 4:13).

When you focus on Jesus instead of your bank account, giving becomes easier. When you remember what He's done for you, generosity flows naturally.

Rachel started giving $100 a month, even though it stretched her budget. "Some months I didn't want to," she admitted. "But I decided to trust God's promises more than my fears. Three years later, I can't imagine living any other way."

The Beauty of Spiritual Compound Interest

Charles Spurgeon put it this way: "By perseverance, the snail reached the ark."

Small, consistent investments compound over time. The same is true spiritually. Consistent giving:

- Builds your faith muscle
- Develops generous habits
- Creates financial margin
- Increases your trust in God
- Multiplies your kingdom impact

Your Steadfastness Challenge

Here's what I want you to do: Pick an amount you can give consistently for the next three months. It doesn't have to be huge. It needs to be sustainable.

Then give that amount, whether you feel like it or not, whether times are good or tough, whether you're motivated or not.

Watch what God does in your heart and in your circumstances.

Prayer for Today: *God, help me be steadfast in my giving just like You are faithful in Your love. Give me the discipline to give consistently, not just emotionally. Help me trust Your promises more than my fears. Please make me a faithful steward who shows up rain or shine. Though I may falter, help me never quit. Amen.*

DAY 6: REVIEW AND REFLECTION

TODAY'S FOCUS: **Applying God's Investment Principles**

We've covered a lot of ground this week. Let's take a step back and see the big picture.

The Five Foundation Stones

Think of these five principles as foundation stones for your financial life:

1. Submission - Surrendering your finances to God's plan.

2. Servanthood - Managing God's resources instead of owning your own.

3. Sowing and Reaping - Investing with eternal perspective.

4. Sacrifice - Giving that costs you something

5. Steadfastness - Consistent, faithful investment over time

The Questions That Matter

Before you move on to Week 2, honestly answer these questions:

Submission: Am I willing to let God guide my financial decisions?

Servanthood: Do I see myself as God's money manager or money's owner?

Sowing and Reaping: Am I investing for this life only or for eternity?

Sacrifice: Does my giving cost me anything, or is it just convenient?

Steadfastness: Am I giving consistently or just emotionally?

The Transformation Promise

Here's what John Bunyan discovered in prison: "In times of affliction, we commonly meet with the sweetest experiences of the love of God."

The same is true when you apply these financial principles. At first, it might feel difficult or scary. But over time, you'll discover that God's way of handling money brings more peace, purpose, and provision than any other approach.

Your Week 1 Commitment

Pick one principle from this week that challenged you the most. Make a specific commitment to apply it this week:

- "I will submit my next major purchase to God in prayer before deciding."
- "I will start seeing myself as God's money manager, not money's owner."
- "I will give something to God's kingdom, even if it's small."
- "I will make a sacrificial gift that actually costs me something."
- "I will commit to giving a specific amount consistently for three months."

The Promise Ahead

Jesus said: "If you abide in My word, you are My disciples indeed. And you shall know the truth, and the truth shall make you free" (John 8:31-32).

> **Financial freedom doesn't come from having more money. It comes from applying God's truth to the money you have.**

Ready for what's next? We're going to discover how these investment principles transform not just your wallet, but your entire life.

Prayer for Today: *God, thank You for showing me Your principles for financial stewardship this week. Help me apply what I've learned, not just understand it. Transform my heart as I transform my habits. Please show me how these principles can bring freedom instead of bondage, joy instead of anxiety. Prepare my heart for what You want to teach me next week. Amen.*

CHAPTER 2
WEEK TWO: INVESTING YOUR LIFE

> ***Memory Verse:*** *"I beseech you therefore, brethren, by the mercies of God, that ye present your bodies a living sacrifice, holy, acceptable unto God, which is your reasonable service." - Romans 12:1*

DAY 7: THE CRUCIFIED LIFE

TODAY'S FOCUS: **Dying to Self to Live for God**

Scripture Reading: Galatians 2:20

Imagine you inherited a business. However, there's a catch: the previous owner has left such a mess that the only way to save the company is to fire the old management team, including yourself as the heir.

You have two choices: fight to stay in control and watch everything crumble, or step aside and let someone competent take over.

That's precisely the choice every Christian faces with their life.

The Management Problem

Before Jesus saved you, you were the CEO of your own life. And let's be honest - you weren't very good at the job.

Charles Spurgeon said it best: "The best of men are men at best."

Your old management style led to:

- Spiritual bankruptcy
- Relationship failures
- Anxiety about the future
- Emptiness despite success
- A growing sense that something was missing

Sound familiar?

The Takeover Offer

Then Jesus made you an offer: "Come to Me, all you who labor and are heavy laden, and I will give you rest" (Matthew 11:28).

But Jesus doesn't just want to be your consultant. He wants to be your CEO. And that means the old management has to go.

Paul figured this out: "I have been crucified with Christ; it is no longer I who live, but Christ lives in me" (Galatians 2:20).

What Crucified Living Looks Like

The crucified life has three requirements, straight from Jesus' mouth:

1. **"Deny himself"** (Luke 9:23) - Stop making decisions based on what you want and start making them based on what God wants.
2. **"Take up his cross"** (Luke 9:23) - Accept the daily choice to serve God instead of yourself.
3. **"Follow Me"** (Luke 9:23) - Let Jesus lead instead of trying to lead Jesus.

The Results of New Management

When you let Jesus take over as CEO of your life, three incredible things happen:

1. **You get peace** (John 16:33) - Not because problems disappear, but because you know who's in control.
2. **You find purpose** (Philippians 3:13-14) - Your life has direction beyond just paying bills and staying entertained.
3. **You please God** (2 Timothy 2:4) - And there's no greater satisfaction than making your Creator smile.

The Money Connection

You might be wondering: "What does this have to do with money?"

Everything!!

When you're the CEO of your life, your money serves your agenda. When Jesus is the CEO, your money serves His agenda.

When you're in charge, you give leftovers to God. When Jesus is in charge, you give firstfruits to God.

When you're running things, you worry about having enough. When Jesus is running things, you trust Him to provide.

Maria's Story

Maria was raising two kids alone after her divorce, working double shifts as a nurse to make ends meet. "Every penny mattered," she said. "I clipped coupons, bought generic everything, and still struggled to pay rent."

When Maria gave her life to Christ, the last thing she wanted to hear about was giving money away. "I felt like God was asking me to jump off a financial cliff," she admitted. But she decided to trust Him with $5 a week - the cost of her coffee habit.

"That $5 taught me that Jesus could be CEO of my finances even when I was broke," Maria said. "I stopped asking, 'How can I stretch this dollar?' and started asking, 'How can I honor God with this dollar?' The peace that came was worth more than the money I gave."

John Newton's Discovery

Newton's words are powerful; he said, "How unspeakably

wonderful to know that all our concerns are held in hands that bled for us."

Newton understood something profound about surrender. When you place your financial battles, your career ambitions, and your relationship struggles into the hands that were pierced for you, everything changes. Those same hands that conquered death can handle your mortgage payment. Those same hands that rose from the grave can resurrect your broken dreams.

Your Move

The crucified life means releasing control of your concerns to the One who controls all things. Newton learned this truth through years of storms - both at sea and in his soul. He discovered that the safest place for your deepest worries is in the grip of grace.

Your concerns become His concerns. Your battles become His battles. Your future becomes His responsibility. This is the freedom that comes when you die to self-management and trust the hands that bled for you.

Stop carrying what Christ wants to carry for you. Those nail-scarred hands are stronger than your white-knuckled grip.

Prayer for Today: *Jesus, I want to live the crucified life. Help me step down as CEO of my life and let You take over. Show me what it means to deny myself, take up my cross, and follow You, especially with my money. I want to please You more than I want to please myself. Make me alive to Your purposes. Amen.*

DAY 8: THE VICTORIOUS LIFE

TODAY'S FOCUS: **Overcoming the Enemies of Generous Living**

Scripture Reading: 1 John 5:4-5

You have enemies. I don't mean your annoying neighbor or your difficult boss. I mean spiritual enemies that are actively working to keep you from living generously.

The good news? Jesus has already defeated them. The even better news? He's given you the weapons to enforce His victory.

Enemy #1: The World

The "world" isn't the planet. It's the system of values that opposes

God. And when it comes to money, the world has three lies it wants you to believe:

1. "You are what you own" - Your worth equals your wealth.
2. "More is always better" - You need the latest, greatest, newest thing to be happy.
3. "Security comes from savings" - The more you hoard, the safer you are.

But Jesus said: "Do not lay up for yourselves treasures on earth ... but lay up for yourselves treasures in heaven" (Matthew 6:19-20).

How to Beat the World: Faith

John tells us: "This is the victory that has overcome the world - our faith" (1 John 5:4).

Faith believes that following God's way of managing money through obedience brings greater joy than the way of the world. (Tithing: The first 10% of your income)

Faith trusts that giving leads to blessing, even when it doesn't make sense mathematically.

Faith says, "I'd rather be poor and generous than rich and stingy."

Enemy #2: The Flesh

Your flesh is your old nature that still wants to sin. When it comes to money, the flesh whispers:

- "You worked hard for that money. You deserve to spend it on yourself."
- "Give later when you have more."
- "God helps those who help themselves."

How to Beat the Flesh: Flee

Paul's strategy for defeating the flesh was simple: "Flee also youthful lusts" (2 Timothy 2:22).

- You don't fight materialism. You flee from it.
- You don't argue with greed. You run from it.
- You don't negotiate with selfishness. You escape it.

Enemy #3: The Devil

Satan's strategy is simple: convince you that generosity is a dangerous thing. He'll whisper: "What if you give and then lose your job?" "What if there's an emergency?" "What if God doesn't come through?"

How to Beat the Devil: Armor

Paul gives us the armor we need: "Put on the whole armor of God, that you may be able to stand against the wiles of the devil" (Ephesians 6:11).

When Satan attacks your giving with fear, you counter with the helmet of salvation, remembering that God saved you and will continue to provide for you.

When he attacks with greed, you counter with the breastplate of righteousness, remembering that generous living is the right way to live.

When he attacks with doubt, you counter with the sword of the Spirit—God's promises about provision and blessing.

The Victory Celebration

George Whitefield, the great evangelist, said: "God had one Son without sin, but He has no sons without suffering."

The victorious life doesn't mean you'll never face financial pressure. It means you'll face it with confidence instead of fear. Victory over the world means you measure success by kingdom impact, not bank account size. Victory over the flesh means you find joy in giving, not just getting. Victory over the devil means you trust God's promises more than your fears.

David's Example

King David understood victorious living. Even though he faced constant threats to his kingdom, he said: "I have been young, and now am old; yet I have not seen the righteous forsaken, nor his descendants begging bread" (Psalm 37:25). David learned that victory over his enemies came through trusting God, not through hoarding wealth.

Your Victory Strategy

Here's how to live victoriously with your money this week:

- **Against the World**: When you're tempted to buy something to impress others, ask: "Will this advance God's kingdom or just my ego?"
- **Against the Flesh**: When you want to keep all your money for yourself, ask: "What would love do in this situation?"
- **Against the Devil**: When you're afraid to give, ask: "What has God promised about taking care of me?"

Prayer for Today: *God, thank You for giving me victory over the world, the flesh, and the devil. Help me enforce that victory in my financial life. When I'm tempted to live like the world, remind me of Your truth. When my flesh wants to be selfish, help me flee to generosity. When Satan attacks with fear, help me stand firm in Your promises. Make me victorious in my giving. Amen.*

DAY 9: THE SPIRIT-FILLED LIFE

TODAY'S FOCUS: **Living Under the Holy Spirit's Financial Guidance**

Scripture Reading: Ephesians 5:18-21

What if I told you that God has given you a personal financial advisor who:

- Never charges a fee
- Never gives bad advice
- Has perfect knowledge of the future
- Actually cares about your well-being
- Has unlimited resources to back up His recommendations

You'd probably want to meet this advisor.

. . .

You already have. His name is the Holy Spirit.

Why Most Christians Ignore Their Best Advisor

The Holy Spirit isn't some mystical force. He's the third person of the Trinity, and Jesus specifically sent Him to guide you into all truth (John 16:13) - including financial truth.

But most Christians make money decisions without ever consulting Him. Why?

1. We don't think God cares about money (again, He talks about it more than heaven and hell combined.)

2. We're afraid of what He might say (usually because we already know we're being selfish.)

3. We don't know how to listen (more on this in a minute.)

The Early Church's Secret

The early church had something we've lost: they made financial decisions as a community, guided by the Holy Spirit.

In Acts 4:32, we read: "Now the multitude of those who believed were of one heart and one soul; neither did anyone say that any of the things he possessed was his own, but they had all things in common."

This wasn't socialism. This was Spirit-led generosity.

How to Be Filled with the Spirit

Paul commands us: "Be filled with the Spirit" (Ephesians 5:18). This isn't a suggestion. It's a requirement. Here's how:

1. Dedication (Romans 12:1) - Decide you want the Holy Spirit to control your finances, not just your Sunday morning emotions.

2. Daily Submission (Luke 11:13) - Every morning, pray: "Holy Spirit, guide my financial decisions today."

3. Dependence (Galatians 5:16) - Throughout the day, pause before financial decisions and ask: "What would the Spirit have me do?"

What Spirit-Filled Giving Looks Like

When you're filled with the Spirit, your relationship with money changes:

You give because you're prompted, not pressured. The Spirit reveals specific needs and opportunities for giving.

You give with joy, not obligation. Generous giving becomes a natural expression of God's love in you.

You give strategically, not randomly. The Spirit helps you discern which ministries and needs to support.

You give proportionally, not equally. The Spirit guides you to give according to your ability and His leading.

John Newton's Spirit-Led Generosity

John Newton gave away most of his income as a pastor, trusting the Holy Spirit to guide his generosity. He wrote: "If two angels were to receive at the same moment a commission from God, one to go down and rule earth's grandest empire, and the other to go and sweep the streets of its meanest village, it would be a matter of entire indifference to each which service fell to his lot." That's Spirit-filled living - being equally willing to give much or little, as the Spirit leads.

The Results of Spirit-Filled Stewardship

When you let the Holy Spirit guide your finances, several beautiful things happen:

Sanctification - You begin to look more like Jesus in your generosity (Galatians 5:22-23).

Soul-winning - Spirit-filled Christians are enabled to win others through their generous example (John 15:16).

Submission - You become teachable and work well with others in ministry (Ephesians 5:21).

Songs - There's a joy in Spirit-led giving that you can't fake or manufacture (Ephesians 5:19).

Jennifer's Story

Jennifer was terrified of giving. "I grew up poor," she said. "The idea of giving money away scared me to death."

But when Jennifer started asking the Holy Spirit to guide her giving, everything changed. "He started small," she told me. "Five dollars here, ten dollars there. But as I obeyed, He grew my faith and my capacity to give. Now I give away 20% of my income, and I've never been happier."

Your Spirit-Filled Challenge

This week, before you make any financial decision - buying groceries, paying bills, making a purchase - pause and ask the Holy Spirit for guidance. You might be surprised by what He shows you.

Prayer for Today: *Holy Spirit, I invite You to fill my life and guide my financial decisions. I don't want to make money choices based on fear, greed, or cultural pressure. I want to make them based on Your wisdom and leading. Help me be sensitive to Your voice and obedient to Your promptings. Fill me with Your generosity. Amen.*

DAY 10: THE FRUITFUL LIFE

TODAY'S FOCUS: **Making Your Money Count for Eternity**

Scripture Reading: John 15:1-8

Let me ask you a question: What's the point of making money if it doesn't make a difference?

Jesus told a story about a man who worked hard, saved money, and built bigger barns to store his wealth. Then God said to him: "Fool! This night your soul will be required of you; then whose will those things be which you have provided?" (Luke 12:20).

That man's life was financially successful but eternally fruitless.

The Investment That Never Loses Value

Jesus said: "I chose you and appointed you that you should go and bear fruit, and that your fruit should remain" (John 15:16). The only investment that produces fruit that "remains" is investment in human souls.

Think about it:

- The stock market will crash
- Real estate will crumble
- Gold will tarnish
- But souls are eternal

When you invest your money in reaching people with the gospel, you're putting your treasure in the only market that's guaranteed never to lose value.

Philip's Fruitful Strategy

In Acts 8, Philip had a thriving ministry in Samaria. Thousands were being saved and healed. Any rational person would have stayed and built on that success. But God told Philip to leave the crowds and go to a desert road to talk to an Ethiopian eunuch. Philip obeyed, led the man to Christ, and that one conversation changed the entire nation of Ethiopia.

The Essentials of Fruitful Living

Philip understood three principles that made his life fruitful:

1. The value of a human soul (Mark 8:36) - "What will it profit a man if he gains the whole world, and loses his own soul?"

2. The command to go (Mark 16:15) - "Go into all the world and preach the gospel to every creature."

3. The resolve to bear fruit (Psalm 126:6) - "He who continually goes forth weeping, bearing seed for sowing, shall doubtless come again with rejoicing, bringing his sheaves with him."

William Carey's Fruitful Vision

William Carey, the father of modern missions, left his comfortable life in England to take the gospel to India. People thought he was crazy. Carey's response: "Expect great things from God; attempt great things for God." Carey invested his life and money in spreading the gospel to India. The result? Thousands came to Christ, the caste system was challenged, and Indian society was transformed.

The Fruitful Investment Portfolio

When you start thinking about money with a fruitful mindset, your investment priorities change:

Instead of asking: "How can I get the best return on my money?"

You ask: "How can I get the best eternal return on my money?"

Instead of asking: "What will make me more secure?"

You ask: "What will make more people secure in Christ?"

Instead of asking: "How can I build wealth for my family?"

You ask: "How can I build God's family?"

The Multiplication Principle

Here's what's impressive about fruitful investing: it multiplies.

When you support missions, you're not just reaching one person - you're reaching everyone that person will reach.

When you invest in children's ministry, you're not just impacting one child—you're impacting everyone that child will influence.

> **When you support church planting, you're not just starting one church - you're starting a movement that could plant hundreds of churches.**

Jake's Reality

Jake graduated from college with $40,000 in student loans and landed his first "real job" making $35,000 as a social worker. "Everyone told me to focus on paying off debt before I even thought about giving," he said.

But Jake's mentor challenged him: "What if God wants to use your giving to build your faith while you pay off debt?" Jake started giving $50 a month to his church's youth ministry, money he "couldn't afford" to give.

"I discovered that God was more concerned about my heart than my debt," Jake said. Three years later, his loans are paid off and he's leading a financial discipleship group at church. "Learning to give sacrificially when I was broke prepared me to give generously now that I have more."

Your Fruitful Challenge

Charles Spurgeon said, "Every Christian is either a missionary or an impostor."

The same is true of your money. It's either on mission for God or it's missing the point.

This week, ask yourself: "If my money could talk, what would it say about the eternal fruit it's producing?"

Then make one financial decision—big or small—that prioritizes souls over stuff.

Prayer for Today: *Jesus, I want my life and my money to bear fruit that remains. Help me see people the way You see them - as souls of infinite value. Please show me how to invest my resources in ways that will matter for eternity. Make my money a tool for reaching others with Your love. Help me prioritize souls over stuff. Amen.*

DAY 11: THE ABUNDANT LIFE

TODAY'S FOCUS: **Experiencing God's Overflow Through Generosity**

Scripture Reading: John 10:10

Jesus said: "I have come that they may have life, and that they may have it more abundantly" (John 10:10). However, what's interesting is that Jesus didn't promise abundant bank accounts as some prosperity pastors preach. He promised an abundant life.

The "abundant life" Jesus promises refers to spiritual abundance, purpose, peace, and joy, not necessarily material abundance. Some of the most spiritually abundant people in history lived with very modest material means.

. . .

What most people miss is this: the abundant life often comes through abundant giving, not abundant getting.

David's Abundance Cycle
King David's life illustrates how abundance works:

Abundance received - God chose David not because of his appearance or abilities, but because of his heart (1 Samuel 16:7).

Abundance revoked - When David sinned with Bathsheba and killed Uriah, he lost the joy and blessing of abundance (2 Samuel 12:9-12).

Abundance restored - When David genuinely repented, God restored the abundant life (Psalm 51:12): "Restore to me the joy of Your salvation."

David learned that abundance isn't about what you accumulate—it's about your relationship with God.

The True Abundance Formula
Most people think:

More Money = More Happiness

But research consistently shows this isn't true. After your basic needs are met, more money doesn't equal more satisfaction.

Jesus taught a different formula:

More Generosity = More Joy

> **"It is more blessed to give than to receive" (Acts 20:35).**

The Essentials of Abundant Living
The abundant life has three characteristics:

1. Duties performed cheerfully (Philippians 2:14-15) - You give joyfully, not grudgingly.

2. Devotion to God (Colossians 3:1) - Your heart is set on heavenly things, not earthly possessions.

3. Determination to live for Christ (Daniel 1:8) - You've resolved to honor God regardless of the cost.

The Abundance Cycle
Here's how God's abundance cycle works:

Abundant life → Abundant joy → Abundant strength → Abundant service → Abundant reward

Let me break this down:

When you live God's way, you experience joy that is not dependent on circumstances. That joy gives you the strength to serve others, even when it's difficult. That service leads to rewards, both now and in eternity. Those rewards enable even more abundant living.

John Bunyan's Abundant Poverty

John Bunyan wrote "Pilgrim's Progress" while in prison for preaching the gospel. He had no money, no freedom, and no earthly comfort. But Bunyan wrote: "I have never lived so cheerfully as I do now - the love of Christ constrains me." Bunyan discovered that abundance isn't about external circumstances—it's about internal reality.

The Counterfeit Abundance

Our culture offers a counterfeit abundance based on:

- Having more stuff
- Experiencing more pleasure
- Achieving more success
- Gaining more recognition

But Jesus offers authentic abundance based on:

- Giving more generously
- Serving more sacrificially
- Loving more unconditionally
- Living more purposefully

Robert's Discovery

Robert had worked for 40 years, saved wisely, and retired with a comfortable nest egg. "I thought I was done giving," he said. "I figured I'd paid my dues and earned the right to enjoy my money."

But Robert felt restless in retirement until his pastor challenged him to think about legacy. "I realized I was living like my story was over, but God wasn't done with me yet," Robert said.

Robert began giving significantly to his church's building fund and mentoring young families about financial stewardship.

"I discovered that my retirement years could be my most generous years. Instead of just spending down my savings, I'm investing in the next generation. It's given me more purpose than golf ever could."

Adoniram Judson's Abundant Investment

Adoniram Judson left the comforts of America and stepped into the unknown for the sake of the Gospel in Burma. His journey was marked by heartbreak and hardship—he buried his wife and children in foreign soil, endured brutal imprisonment, and often lived in poverty.

Yet through it all, Judson held to a fierce confidence in God's providence. He once said:

"There is no success without sacrifice. If you succeed without sacrifice, it is because someone has suffered before you. If you sacrifice without success, it is because someone will succeed after you." Judson didn't measure success in comfort, numbers, or applause. He measured it in faithfulness and eternity.

His life was a seed, sown with tears, that produced a harvest.

His abundant investment led to abundant fruit: thousands came to Christ, the Burmese Bible was translated, and churches were planted in a land once resistant to the Gospel.

Judson teaches us that Gospel fruit often grows from the soil of suffering, but no sacrifice for Christ is ever wasted.

Your Abundance Choice

You have a choice to make: Will you pursue the world's counterfeit abundance or God's authentic abundance? The world's abundance says: "Get all you can, can all you get, and sit on the can." God's abundance says: "Give all you can, serve all you can, and trust Me for the outcome." Which sounds more appealing to your soul?

Prayer for Today: *Jesus, I want the abundant life You promised. Please help me understand that abundance comes through giving, not getting. Transform my definition of success from accumulation to generosity. Give me the joy that comes from abundant living, the strength that comes from abundant service, and the reward that comes from abundant investment in Your kingdom. Amen.*

DAY 12: REVIEW AND REFLECTION

TODAY'S FOCUS: **Integrating the Life Investment Journey**

This week, we've journeyed through five stages of spiritual life investment. Let's pause and see how they fit together.

The Progressive Journey

Notice that these stages build on each other:

1. Crucified Life - You die to your selfish financial desires.
2. Victorious Life - You overcome the enemies of generous living.
3. Spirit-Filled Life - You let God guide your financial decisions.
4. Fruitful Life - You invest for eternal impact.

5. Abundant Life - You experience God's overflow through generosity.

You can't skip stages.

You can't live victoriously until you've died to self. You can't be Spirit-filled until you've learned victory. You can't be fruitful until you're Spirit-filled. You can't experience abundance until you're fruitful.

Charles Spurgeon's Progressive Wisdom

Charles Spurgeon understood this progression: "The Lord gets His best soldiers out of the highlands of affliction." Spurgeon learned that spiritual maturity comes through stages, not shortcuts. The same is true of financial maturity.

Where Are You in the Journey? Honestly assess where you are in this progression:

Crucified Life: Have I surrendered my finances to God, or am I still trying to be the CEO of my money?

Victorious Life: Am I overcoming the world's materialism, my flesh's selfishness, and Satan's fear-mongering?

Spirit-Filled Life: Do I consult the Holy Spirit before making financial decisions, or do I follow my impulses?

Fruitful Life: Is my money producing eternal fruit, or is it just producing temporary comfort?

Abundant Life: Am I experiencing the joy that comes from a life of generosity?

The Honest Assessment

Don't be discouraged if you're not yet at the "abundant life" stage. John Newton said: "I am not what I ought to be, I am not what I want to be, I am not what I hope to be in another world; but still I am not what I once used to be."

Growth is a process, not a destination.

Your Next Step

Instead of trying to jump to the end, focus on your next step:

- If you're learning to crucify selfishness, focus on one area where you can die to self this week.
- If you're fighting for victory, choose one enemy (world, flesh, or devil) to resist specifically.
- If you're growing in Spirit-filled living, commit to consulting God before financial decisions.
- If you're pursuing fruitfulness, make one investment in eternal souls.
- If you're experiencing abundance, find someone to encourage in their journey.

The Promise of Progression

William Carey understood that spiritual progress requires both divine guidance and practical wisdom. He said, "To know the will of God, we need an open Bible and an open map." Carey combined scriptural truth with real-world application.

The same is true of your financial spiritual journey. You need God's Word to guide your heart and practical wisdom to guide your steps. Consistency beats intensity. Small steps forward beat significant steps backward.

Week 2 Commitment

Based on this week's lessons, complete this statement:

"This week, I will take one specific step forward in my journey by

____

____."

Examples:

- "Asking the Holy Spirit to guide one major financial decision"
- "Making one sacrificial gift to advance God's kingdom"
- "Choosing joy over anxiety when I pay my bills"
- "Giving away something I've been hoarding"

Looking Ahead

Next, we'll discover how these personal transformations impact your relationship with the local church. You'll learn why the church isn't just one of many good places to invest your money - it's God's primary vehicle for advancing His kingdom on earth.

Prayer for Today: *God, thank You for showing me the progressive journey of life investment this week. Please help me be patient with myself while staying committed to growth. Show me my next step and give me the courage to take it. Don't let me settle for where I am, but don't let me be discouraged by where I'm not. Keep me moving forward in Your grace. Amen.*

CHAPTER 3
WEEK THREE: INVESTING IN THE CHURCH

> ***Memory Verse:*** *"Not forsaking the assembling of ourselves together, as the manner of some is; but exhorting one another: and so much the more, as ye see the day approaching." - Hebrews 10:25*

DAY 13: HONORING THE TRUTHS OF THE LOCAL CHURCH

TODAY'S FOCUS: **Understanding What Makes the Church Worth Your Investment**

Scripture Reading: 1 Timothy 3:15

Let me guess: you've been hurt by a church.

Maybe a pastor was greedy. Maybe members were hypocritical. Perhaps leaders made poor financial decisions. Possibly you've seen enough scandals on the news that you're skeptical about investing in any church.

I get it. Jesus gets it, too.

Jesus had stronger words for religious leaders who mishandled money than for almost anyone else. He called them "whitewashed tombs" and "children of hell" (Matthew 23:15, 27).

But here's what Jesus also said: "I will build My church, and the gates of Hades shall not prevail against it" (Matthew 16:18).

> **Despite the failures of some churches and some leaders, Jesus is still building His church. And He wants you to be part of it.**

Understanding What You're Investing In

Before you invest in any company, you research it, right? You want to know:

- Who owns it?
- Who runs it?
- What's their business plan?
- What's their track record?

Let's do the same with the church.

The Owner: Jesus Christ

Denominations, pastors, or boards don't own the church. Jesus owns it.

Paul reminds church leaders: "Be shepherds of the church of God, which he bought with his own blood" (Acts 20:28).

Every time you invest in a Bible-believing church, you're investing in something Jesus purchased with His life. That's the ultimate ownership guarantee.

The Manager: Your Pastor

God has placed pastors as shepherds over local churches. That doesn't make them perfect, but it does make them responsible.

The Bible says: "Obey those who rule over you, and be submissive, for they watch out for your souls, as those who must give account" (Hebrews 13:17).

Your pastor will answer to God for how he leads your church. That's a sobering responsibility that most pastors take seriously.

God's Plan: The Great Commission

Every legitimate church exists for three purposes:

1. **Teaching pure doctrine** (1 Timothy 1:3) - Helping people understand what God says.
2. **Proclaiming the Gospel** (Mark 16:15) - Helping lost people find salvation.
3. **Protecting the faith** (Jude 3) - Helping believers stay firm against false teaching.

> **If a church isn't doing these three things, it's not really a church - it's just a religious social club.**

Charles Spurgeon's Church Vision

Charles Spurgeon pastored the largest church in the world in his day, but he never lost sight of the church's purpose: "The Gospel is like a caged lion. It does not need to be defended, it just needs to be let out of its cage."

Spurgeon's church focused on letting the Gospel loose through preaching, missions, and church planting. The result? Thousands were saved, and hundreds of churches were planted.

But What About Imperfect Churches?

You might be thinking: "That sounds great in theory, but my church isn't perfect."

Here's a newsflash: **No church is perfect.** John Newton said, "If I might trust my own heart, and if I might hope to stand in my strength, I might venture out; but since I know my weakness, I choose to stay by the fountain."

The church is full of imperfect people led by imperfect pastors serving a perfect Savior.

That doesn't excuse sin or poor leadership. However, it does mean you shouldn't expect perfection from an institution comprised of people in the process.

What to Look For

When evaluating whether a church is worth your investment, ask:

1. Do they teach the Bible accurately? - Not just use it as a jumping-off point for self-help talks.
2. Do they preach the Gospel clearly? - Not just assume everyone is already saved.
3. Do they love people genuinely? - Not just put on a show for Sunday mornings.
4. Do they handle money transparently? - Not hide financial information from members.

Your Investment Matters

When you find a church that's genuinely trying to fulfill God's purposes, your investment matters enormously.

Your giving supports Bible teaching that transforms lives. Your serving creates an atmosphere where the Gospel can be heard. Your presence encourages other believers to stay faithful.

Prayer for Today: *Jesus, thank You for purchasing the church with Your blood and calling me to be part of it. Help me find a church that's genuinely committed to Your purposes. Give me wisdom to discern the difference between imperfection and unfaithfulness. Show me how to invest in Your church in ways that honor You and advance Your kingdom. Amen.*

DAY 14: PUTTING YOUR TRUST IN THE LOCAL CHURCH

TODAY'S FOCUS: **Believing God Works Through His Church**

Scripture Reading: Ephesians 4:11-16

Here's a question that might surprise you: **What's the most criticized institution in America that Jesus personally promised to build and protect?**

Answer: The local church.

Everyone has an opinion about the church. Politicians criticize it. The media mocks it. Even Christians complain about it.

But Jesus said: "I will build My church, and the gates of Hades shall not prevail against it" (Matthew 16:18).

So the question is: Will you trust Jesus' opinion or popular opinion?

Trusting the Church's Manual

Every successful organization operates by a manual. The church's manual is the Bible.

Here's what Scripture does for the church:

- **Sanctifies it** (Ephesians 5:26) - The Word cleanses and purifies the church
- **Preserves it** (Psalm 119:89) - God's Word endures forever, so churches built on it endure too
- **Directs it** (2 Timothy 3:16) - Scripture guides all church decisions

> **When you invest in a church that's committed to biblical authority, you're investing in something with a 2,000-year track record of success.**

Trusting the Church's Mission

God has given His church a clear mission: make disciples (Matthew 28:19). This breaks down into two parts:

1. Evangelize the lost (Acts 1:8) - Reach people who don't know Jesus

2. Edify the saints (Ephesians 4:12) - Build up people who do know Jesus

Every ministry in a healthy church should somehow connect to this mission. Children's ministry? Teaching kids about Jesus and building up believing families. Music ministry? Reaching hearts with the Gospel and encouraging believers to worship. Benevolence ministry? Showing Christ's love to those in need.

Trusting the Church's Methods

God has established specific methods for accomplishing His work:

Personal evangelism (Acts 5:42) - The most effective outreach happens life-to-life, not program-to-program.

Biblical preaching (1 Corinthians 1:21) - God chose the "foolishness of preaching" to save people.

Community life (Acts 2:42-47) - People are drawn to Christ when they see an authentic Christian community.

William Carey's Trust

William Carey trusted God's calling so profoundly that he left behind the safety of home. Carey wasn't driven by applause or success. His greatest fear wasn't failure. It was wasting his life on things that didn't matter to God. He said, "I am not afraid of failure; I am afraid of succeeding at things that don't matter." He believed God would work through the local church, and he gave his time, talent, and treasure to see that happen in India. Carey's life wasn't comfortable, but it was consecrated. And God used it mightily.

But What About Church Scandals?

You might be thinking: "That's nice, but what about all the church scandals I see on the news?"

Here's the thing: Scandals don't disprove God's plan for the church any more than medical malpractice disproves God's plan for healing.

When a doctor commits malpractice, you don't stop trusting medicine - you find a better doctor.

When a church leader fails morally or financially, you don't stop trusting the church; you find a better one.

John Bunyan's Church Commitment

John Bunyan was imprisoned for 12 years for preaching without a license. He could have given up on the church and just had private faith.

Instead, Bunyan wrote: "The church is the pillar and ground of the truth." Even in prison, he continued to trust God's plan for the local church.

Your Trust Investment

When you trust the local church enough to invest in it, several things happen:

You become part of something bigger than yourself - Your life connects to God's global mission.

You multiply your impact - Your gifts combine with others' gifts to accomplish more than any of you could alone.

You experience biblical community - You get to live life alongside other people who share your values.

You contribute to something eternal - Local churches have been the primary vehicle for Gospel advancement for 2,000 years.

The Trust Challenge

Maybe you've been hurt by a church. Perhaps you're skeptical about organized religion. Maybe you prefer to "go it alone" spiritually. But consider this: Jesus didn't design Christianity to be a solo sport. He created it to be a team effort. And the local church, despite its imperfections, is still God's team for advancing His kingdom on earth.

Prayer for Today: *God, help me trust Your plan for the local church even when individual churches and leaders disappoint me. Show me a church that's genuinely committed to Your Word, Your mission, and Your methods. Give me faith to invest in that church even when it's not perfect. Please help me be part of the solution, rather than part of the criticism. Amen.*

DAY 15: GIVING YOUR TIME, TREASURE, AND TALENT

TODAY'S FOCUS: **The Three-Legged Stool of Church Investment**

Scripture Reading: 1 Corinthians 12:4-7

Imagine you have a three-legged stool. What happens if you remove one leg?

The stool falls over.

> **Your investment in the local church is like a three-legged stool: Time, Treasure, and Talent. Remove any leg, and your investment becomes unstable.**

Leg 1: Your Time

Time is your most valuable resource because it's the only thing you can't get more of. When you give your time to the church, you're saying: "This matters enough to me that I'm willing to invest my life in it."

The Bible says believers should:

• **Work for the local church** (1 Thessalonians 1:3) - Set aside specific hours each week to serve.

• **Worship in the local church** (Acts 2:46) - Prioritize gathering with other believers.

• **Witness through the local church** (Philippians 2:15-16) - Connect your personal evangelism to your church family.

But I'm So Busy

I hear this all the time: "I'd love to serve, but I'm just so busy."

Here's the truth: You're not too busy. Your priorities are just not aligned with God.

Here is the truth, we make time for what we value. If you value Netflix more than God's kingdom, you'll binge-watch shows instead of serving at church.

Jesus said: "Look at the birds of the air, for they neither sow nor reap nor gather into barns; yet your heavenly Father feeds them. Are you not of more value than they?" (Matthew 6:26).

Notice the order: Kingdom first, other things second.

Leg 2: Your Treasure

Let's talk about money. I know this makes some people uncomfortable, but Jesus spoke about money more than heaven and hell combined. Why? Because your money reveals your heart.

The Bible teaches three principles about giving your treasure:

1. **Proper attitude** (2 Corinthians 8:12) - "God loves a willing mind to give." Give joyfully, not grudgingly.
2. **Proper action** (1 Corinthians 16:2) - "On the first day of the week let each one of you lay something aside, storing up as he may prosper, that there be no collections when I come." Give systematically, not randomly.
3. **Proper appreciation** (2 Corinthians 9:15) - "Thanks be to God for His indescribable gift!" Give gratefully, not reluctantly.
4. **Proper Proportion** (2 Corinthians 9:6-7)

These verses encourage regular, proportionate giving, emphasizing cheerful and voluntary giving rather than a strict 10% rule. The 10% tithe is the starting point in the Old Testament, and Jesus builds on it.

But What About My Bills?

"I'd love to give more, but I've got bills to pay."

I understand. But consider this: Jesus promised, "*It is more blessed to give than to receive*" (*Acts 20:35*). He didn't say, "*Give after you pay all your bills.*" He said generous giving brings greater blessings than anxious hoarding.

Charles Spurgeon's Treasure Principle

Charles Spurgeon gave away most of his income despite pastoring the largest church in the world. He said, "Giving is the thermometer of our love." Spurgeon understood that how we handle money reveals how much we trust God.

Leg 3: Your Talent

God has given every believer spiritual gifts for one purpose: to serve the local church.

These gifts come from the Holy Spirit and are necessary in the local church (1 Corinthians 12:11).

The believer should use those talents (1 Timothy 4:14) - Don't neglect your gifts.

The local church benefits when believers use their talents (1 Corinthians 12:7) - When everyone serves, everyone wins.

But I Don't Have Any Talents!

That's not true. You may not yet know what your talents are, but you possess them.

The best way to discover your talents? Start serving somewhere and see what God does through you.

Adoniram Judson's Talent Investment

Adoniram Judson was one of America's first missionaries to the foreign field. He gave up a promising career to take his linguistic talents to Burma. The result? Judson translated the entire Bible into Burmese, established churches throughout Burma, and saw thousands come to Christ. Judson could have utilized his talents to become wealthy in the United States. Instead, he invested them in God's kingdom and changed an entire nation.

The Three-Legged Balance

Here's what's interesting: these three investments work together. When you give your time, you discover your talents. When you use your abilities, you become more generous with your treasure. When you give your treasure, you become more committed to your time.

Michelle's Three-Legged Story

Michelle started by volunteering one hour a week in the nursery (time). As she served, she discovered she had a gift for working with children (talent). Her love for the ministry made her want to support it financially (treasure). Now Michelle leads the children's ministry, gives 15% of her income to the church, and says it's the most fulfilling thing she's ever done.

Your Three-Legged Assessment

Honestly evaluate your church investment:

- **Time**: How many hours per week do you invest in church activities? (worship, serving, fellowship)
- **Treasure**: What percentage of your income do you give to your church?
- **Talent**: How are you using your gifts to strengthen your church family?

If any leg is missing, your church investment is unstable.

Prayer for Today: *God, help me give my time, treasure, and talents to Your church. Please show me where I'm strong and where I need to grow. Help me see that my three-fold investment isn't about what the church needs from me, but about what I need from the church - purpose, community, and the joy of serving You alongside others. Amen.*

DAY 16: LIVING YOUR TESTIMONY THROUGH THE CHURCH

TODAY'S FOCUS: **Making Your Life a Witness for Christ**

Scripture Reading: Matthew 5:13-16

What if I told you that your reputation in your community depends more on your church than your job?

Here's what I mean: When people find out you're a Christian, they don't judge Christianity based on what you do at work. They judge it based on what your church does in the community.

That's why your testimony is inseparable from your church's testimony.

The Salt and Light Principle

Jesus said: "You are the salt of the earth ... You are the light of the world" (Matthew 5:13-14).

Notice: Jesus didn't say you should try to be salt and light. He said you are salt and light.

But here's the catch: Salt only works when it's applied to something. Light only works when it shines in darkness.

> **Your testimony only works when it's connected to something bigger than yourself.**

Your Testimony Should Praise God

A biblical testimony has three components:

- **1. Praise Him as Creator** (Psalm 139:14) - Thank God for the life He's given you.
- **2. Praise Him as Deliverer** (Colossians 1:13) - Remember what He saved you from.
- **3. Praise Him as Sustainer** (1 Peter 5:7) - Acknowledge His daily provision.

However, here's what many Christians often overlook:

Individual testimonies are powerful, but corporate testimonies are unstoppable.

When one person praises God, people notice. When an entire church praises God through its service to the community, people pay attention.

Your Testimony Should Point to Christ

Paul said, "I determined not to know anything among you except Jesus Christ and Him crucified" (1 Corinthians 2:2).

Your personal story is interesting, but it's not the main point. Christ is the main point.

This is where the local church becomes crucial. Your testimony might lead someone to be interested in Jesus. But the local church is where they can:

- Hear the Gospel clearly explained
- See how Christ lived out in community
- Find support for their spiritual growth
- Discover their purpose in God's kingdom

Your Testimony Should Draw Power from the Holy Spirit

Jesus promised: "You shall receive power when the Holy Spirit has come upon you; and you shall be witnesses to Me" (Acts 1:8). Individual Christians filled with the Spirit are powerful. But groups of Spirit-filled Christians working together through a local church ... that's how movements start.

John Newton's Church-Connected Testimony
Newton could have just been known as the former slave trader who wrote "Amazing Grace." Instead, he became a pastor and connected his testimony to a local church.

The result? Newton's story didn't just inspire individuals - it helped launch the abolitionist movement in England. His church became a center for social reform that ultimately contributed to the abolition of slavery in the British Empire.

George Whitefield's Community Impact
George Whitefield could have just been a traveling evangelist. Instead, he helped establish churches everywhere he preached. Whitefield understood that individual conversions needed to be connected to church communities for lasting impact. His ministry contributed to the Great Awakening, a movement that transformed entire communities across America and England.

The Testimony Multiplication Effect
When you connect your testimony to a local church, amazing things happen:

- **Your story becomes part of a bigger story** - Instead of just your transformation, people see how God transforms communities.
- **Your influence multiplies** - You reach people directly, but your church reaches people you'll never meet.

- **Your legacy continues** - You'll die someday, but the church you invest in can continue your testimony for generations.

The Community Reputation

Here's something most Christians don't think about: Your church's reputation in the community affects the effectiveness of your testimony. If your church is known for:

• **Financial transparency** - People trust your personal integrity.

• **Genuine love** - People believe your message about God's love.

• **Community service** - People see your faith as practical, not just theoretical.

• **Biblical truth** - People know where you stand and why.

But What If My Church Has a Bad Reputation?

First, make sure the reputation truly reflects your church's qualities. If there are genuine issues, take steps to foster positive change through revitalization and renewal, or consider exploring a more vibrant church community.

But if your church is being criticized for standing on biblical truth, remember what Jesus said: "Blessed are you when they revile and persecute you, and say all kinds of evil against you falsely for My sake" (Matthew 5:11).

Your Testimony Investment

When you invest in your local church, you're investing in your testimony. Every dollar you give, every hour you serve, every talent you use makes your church a better platform for the Gospel.

And when your church has a strong reputation in the community, your personal testimony carries more weight.

Prayer for Today: *Jesus, help me understand that my testimony and my church's testimony are connected. Show me how to invest in my church in ways that strengthen both. Make my life and my church a clear witness to Your love and truth in our community. Help people see You through us. Amen.*

DAY 17: EXPRESSING YOUR THANKS TO YOUR CHURCH

TODAY'S FOCUS: **Cultivating a Heart of Gratitude**

Scripture Reading: 1 Thessalonians 5:18

When was the last time you said "thank you" to your church?

I don't mean a quick "thanks" to the pastor after the sermon. I mean genuine gratitude for what your church has done in your life and community.

> **Most of us are quicker to criticize our church than thank it.**

But gratitude is the foundation of generous investment.

Thanks to God's Providence

Take a moment to think about how God has worked through your church:

- **Salvation** - Maybe you or someone you love found Christ through your church's ministry.
- **Sanctification** - How has your church's teaching helped you grow spiritually?
- **Service** - What opportunities to serve others has your church provided?
- **Support** - How has your church family helped you through difficult times?

John Newton's Gratitude

John Newton never got over grace. He saw his life as a beautiful miracle, gratefully recognizing how the mercy of Jesus Christ had completely transformed him from being a former slave trader. He often took a moment to reflect on just how astonishing it was that he had been saved.

In one of his letters, he wrote: "If I ever reach heaven, I expect to find three wonders there: first, to meet some I had not thought to see there; second, to miss some I had expected to see there; and third, the greatest wonder of all—to find myself there."

This kind of humility fueled Newton's gratitude. It didn't make him passive—it moved him to action.

He poured himself into the local church, discipled young leaders, wrote hymns, and faithfully preached the Gospel. His legacy was not built on talent or strategy—but on a profound sense of awe that he had been found by grace.

Newton's life reminds us that when you realize how far God has brought you, generosity and service aren't a burden; they're a joyful response.

Thanks to God's Preacher

Your pastor has made sacrifices you probably don't know about:

- **Financial sacrifice** - Most pastors could earn more money in other careers.
- **Family sacrifice** - Pastors' families live in fishbowls and share their husbands/fathers with the congregation.
- **Personal sacrifice** - Pastors carry emotional burdens for their congregation that would crush most people.

Adoniram Judson's Pastor Heart

Judson left America to be a missionary to Burma. In 40 years of ministry, he saw his wife and several children die, was imprisoned and tortured, and lived in poverty. But Judson lived by a simple philosophy: "The motto of every missionary, whether preacher, printer, or schoolmaster, ought to be 'Devoted for Life'." That's a pastor's heart - one completely committed to lifelong service regardless of personal cost.

Thanks to God's People

Your church can't function without volunteers:

- **Teachers** who prepare lessons and invest in others' spiritual growth
- **Musicians** who use their talents to lead worship
- **Servants** who set up chairs, clean bathrooms, and do a thousand invisible tasks
- **Givers** who provide the financial resources for the ministry

Charles Spurgeon's People Appreciation

Charles Spurgeon pastored a church of over 5,000 members, but he never forgot to appreciate the faithful servants who made ministry possible. Spurgeon said, "A church is not a gallery for the exhibition of eminent Christians, but a school for the education of imperfect ones." He understood that ministry happens through ordinary people doing extraordinary things for God.

The Gratitude-Generosity Connection

Here's something researchers have discovered: grateful people tend to be more generous. When you appreciate what your church has done for you, you naturally want to give back. When you recognize the sacrifices others have made, you're more willing to make sacrifices yourself. When you see God's faithfulness through your church, you trust Him enough to invest more.

But What If My Church Isn't Perfect?

Every church has problems. Every pastor makes mistakes. Every congregation has difficult people. But William Carey never let opposition deter him from faithful service. He understood that ministry requires both vision and persistence. Carey once observed: "To know the will of God, we need an open Bible and an open map." He combined scriptural wisdom with practical strategy, serving God faithfully regardless of the circumstances, seeing service as a privilege rather than a burden.

That's the heart of gratitude—not glorifying the pain, but glorifying the privilege of being used by God. Carey reminds us: You don't have to be the most gifted. You just have to keep going, with a grateful heart and a Gospel-centered focus.

Practical Gratitude

Here are some ways to express gratitude to your church:

- **Write a note** to your pastor thanking him for a specific sermon or ministry.
- **Volunteer** for a ministry that blesses you instead of just consuming it.
- **Give generously** as an expression of thanksgiving, not obligation.
- **Speak positively** about your church to others in the community.

- **Pray specifically** for your church leaders and ministries.

The Gratitude Challenge

This week, make a list of 10 specific things your church has done that you're grateful for. Then pick one and express your gratitude tangibly.

Maybe it's a financial gift to a ministry that blessed you. Perhaps it's a thank-you note to a volunteer who serves faithfully. Maybe it's offering to help with a church project. Maybe it's bringing a friend to experience what you're grateful for.

Prayer for Today: *God, forgive me for being quicker to criticize my church than to thank it. Help me see all the ways You've worked through my church in my life and community. Fill my heart with gratitude that leads to generous investment. Show me specific ways to express my appreciation this week. Thank You for the privilege of being part of Your church. Amen.*

DAY 18: REVIEW AND REFLECTION

TODAY'S FOCUS: **Solidifying Your Church Investment Strategy**

This week, we've explored why the local church deserves your investment. Let's review the key truths and make practical commitments.

The Five Foundations of Church Investment

1. **Honor the Church's Truths** - Understanding the Owner (Jesus), Leadership (pastors), and Purpose (Great Commission)
2. **Trust the Church's Function** - Believing God works through the church's manual (Bible), mission (discipleship), and methods (personal ministry)
3. **Give Your Three-Fold Investment** - Contributing

your time, treasure, and talents

4. Live Your Testimony - Connecting your witness to your church's community impact

5. Express Your Gratitude - Appreciating God's providence, the preacher, and the people

Addressing Common Objections

Maybe this week has brought up some objections in your mind:

"I've been hurt by churches before." Remember: You don't reject medicine because some doctors commit malpractice. Find a healthier church. Don't give up on the church.

"I can worship God without going to church." You can, but God designed Christianity as a team sport. You're missing community, accountability, and the power of corporate ministry.

"Churches just want my money." Some do. Find a church that wants your heart and has earned your trust through transparency and biblical faithfulness.

"I don't have time to get involved." You make time for what you value. The question is: Do you value God's kingdom enough to invest your life in it?

William Carey's Church Commitment

William Carey could have been a "lone ranger" missionary. Instead, he planted churches everywhere he went because he understood that sustainable kingdom impact happens through local churches.

Remember Carey's conviction: "I will go down, if you will hold the rope." Carey understood that effective ministry requires both personal courage and community support. That's impossible to do alone. It requires the support, encouragement, and partnership of a church family.

Your Church Investment Assessment

Rate yourself honestly in each area (1-5 scale) - (1 - Rarely | 2 - Occasionally | 3 - Sometimes | 4 - Often | 5 - Consistently)

1. **Church Honor**: Do I understand and appreciate my church's divine ownership, pastoral leadership, and biblical purpose? ___
2. **Church Trust**: Do I believe God works through my church's commitment to Scripture, discipleship, and personal ministry? ___
3. **Time Investment**: Am I consistently investing my time in worship, service, and fellowship? ___
4. **Financial Investment**: Am I giving regularly and generously to support my church's ministry? ___
5. **Talent Investment**: Am I using my gifts and abilities to strengthen my church family? ___
6. **Testimony Connection**: Is my personal witness connected to and supported by my church community? ___

7. **Gratitude Expression**: Do I actively appreciate and thank God for the ministry of my church? ___

Total Score: ____ / 35

1. Where am I strong? Where can I grow?

2. What's one practical step I can take this week to deepen my investment?

Your Church Investment Plan

Based on this assessment, what specific steps will you take?

This Week: What's one thing you can do this week to invest more fully in your church?
This Month: What's one area where you can significantly increase your investment?
This Year: What's one big goal for your church involvement?

The Spurgeon Standard
Charles Spurgeon said, "A Bible that's falling apart usually belongs to someone who isn't." The same principle applies to church investment: A life that's disconnected from the local church usually belongs to someone whose faith is falling apart.

Looking Ahead

Next, we'll expand our perspective beyond the local church to see how your investments today impact eternity. You'll discover why the choices you make with your money now determine your experience forever.

Prayer for Today: *God, thank You for the privilege of being part of Your church. Help me see my investment in the local church not as an obligation but as an opportunity. Show me specific ways to increase my time, treasure, and talent investment. Use my church to reach our community and strengthen believers for faithful service. Make me a blessing to my church family. Amen.*

CHAPTER 4

WEEK FOUR: INVESTING IN THE FUTURE

> ***Memory Verse:*** *"So is he that lays up treasure for himself, and is not rich toward God." - Luke 12:21*

DAY 19: INVESTING IN THE FUTURE AVOIDS WRATH

TODAY'S FOCUS: **Understanding the Stakes of Your Financial Choices**

Scripture Reading: Luke 12:13-21

Let me tell you a story Jesus told about a man who thought he had life figured out.

This guy was successful by every measure that matters to most people. He worked hard, made smart investments, and accumulated wealth. He was so successful that he had to build bigger storage facilities for all his stuff.

Then he made a plan: "I'll take early retirement, travel the world, and enjoy life."

That night, God said to him: "Fool! This night your soul will be required of you; then whose will those things be which you have provided?" (Luke 12:20).

The man spent his whole life building wealth that couldn't save him and accumulating treasures that couldn't follow him.

The Reality of God's Judgement
This may make people uncomfortable, but it's true: God is indeed angry about sin.

Not moody, angry. Not petty angry. But righteously angry about the evil that destroys His creation and hurts His children.

And here's what Jesus taught: How you handle money reveals your relationship with God.

Escaping God's Judgement

1. Receive Salvation (John 3:36)
"He who believes in the Son has everlasting life; and he who does not believe the Son shall not see life, but the wrath of God abides on him."

Your first and most crucial investment must be placing your faith in Jesus Christ. No amount of money can buy salvation, but no amount of money matters without it.

2. Render Service (Hebrews 13:15-16)

""Therefore by Him let us continually offer the sacrifice of praise to God, that is, the fruit of our lips, giving thanks to His name. But do not forget to do good and to share, for with such sacrifices God is well pleased."

Once you're saved, God expects faithful service in response to His grace. This includes how you handle the money He entrusts to you.

3. Reach Souls (2 Corinthians 5:11)

"Knowing, therefore, the terror of the Lord, we persuade men."

The most important investment you can make is in helping others escape God's wrath by finding salvation in Christ.

John Newton's Wrath-to-Grace Story

Newton was a slave trader, profiting from human misery. If anyone deserved God's wrath, it was Newton.

But God saved him, and Newton spent the rest of his life investing in helping others escape the wrath he had escaped. He wrote "Amazing Grace" and played a key role in the movement to abolish slavery in England.

Newton understood that escaping God's wrath comes with a responsibility to help others escape it as well.

The Money Connection

You might be wondering: "What does avoiding God's wrath have to do with money?"

Everything!

Remember, Jesus said: "You cannot serve God and mammon" (Matthew 6:24). "Mammon" means wealth or material possessions.

When you live for money instead of God, you're positioning yourself as God's enemy. When you use money for God's purposes, you're positioning yourself as God's ally.

The Urgency Factor

The rich man in Jesus' story thought he had unlimited time to enjoy his wealth. He was wrong.

You don't know how much time you have left.

Every day you delay investing in God's kingdom is a day you miss building eternal wealth.

Every dollar you spend on temporary pleasure is a dollar you can't invest in permanent treasure.

Every opportunity you skip to serve God is an opportunity you'll never get back.

William Carey's Urgent Investment

Carey was a shoe cobbler who could have lived a comfortable life in England. But he understood the urgency of reaching souls before it's too late. His commitment wasn't built on emotion but on conviction. Carey once said: "Prayer—secret, fervent, believing prayer—lies at the root of all personal godliness." He left everything to become a missionary to India, and his investment in souls helped thousands escape God's wrath and find eternal life.

The Eternal Perspective

Spurgeon put it this way: "You have not lived today until you have done something for someone who can never repay you." When you invest your money in helping people find Christ, you're doing something for them they can never repay - helping them escape eternal wrath and find everlasting life.

Your Wrath-Avoidance Investment Strategy

Here are three questions to ask about every financial decision:

1. Does this investment advance God's kingdom or oppose it?

2. Does this spending help people find Christ or distract them from Him?

3. Will this choice matter in eternity or only in time?

The Bottom Line

You're going to invest your money somewhere. You're going to spend your time on something. You're going to use your talents for some purpose.

The question is, will your investments help people escape God's wrath or ignore it?

Prayer for Today: *God, thank You for saving me from Your wrath through Jesus Christ. Please help me understand the urgency of reaching others before it's too late. Please show me how to invest my money in ways that help people find salvation and escape eternal judgment. Make me a faithful steward who uses resources to reach souls, not just to accumulate stuff. Amen.*

DAY 20: INVESTING IN THE FUTURE IS WISE

TODAY'S FOCUS: **Making Smart Eternal Decisions**

Scripture Reading: Matthew 25:1-13

Here's a question every investor should ask: What good is an excellent return if you don't live long enough to enjoy it?

Most financial planning focuses on this life only. Save for retirement. Build wealth. Leave an inheritance.

But what if there's more to life than the 70-80 years you spend on earth?

Jesus told a story about ten women who were invited to a wedding.

Five were wise and brought extra oil for their lamps. Five were foolish and only got what they thought they needed.

When the bridegroom was delayed, the foolish women ran out of oil. They missed the wedding because they didn't plan for a longer timeline than expected.

Jesus' point: Wise people prepare for longer than they expect to wait.

Human Wisdom vs. God's Wisdom

The world's wisdom says:

- Get all you can while you can
- You only live once, so enjoy it now
- The person with the most toys wins
- Security comes from accumulation

God's wisdom says:

- Give all you can while you can
- You only die once, so prepare for what's next
- The person with the most souls wins
- Security comes from God's promises

1 Corinthians 1:20 asks: "Has not God made foolish the wisdom of this world?"

The Planning-Ahead Principle

Wise people plan forward. They:

- **See the results of sin and avoid it** (Proverbs 22:3)
- **See the results of righteousness and pursue it** (Proverbs 11:19)

When it comes to money, this means asking: "What are the long-term consequences of this financial decision?" Buying a bigger house might bring temporary pleasure, but eternal debt. Giving to missions might bring temporary sacrifice but eternal reward.

Charles Spurgeon's Wise Investment

Spurgeon was offered huge sums of money to tour America as a celebrity preacher. He turned them all down. Instead, Spurgeon invested his income in training preachers, supporting missions, and helping the poor. He died with almost no money but had trained thousands of ministers who reached millions of souls.

Which was wiser: accumulating wealth or accumulating souls?

The Wisdom Rewards

God promises specific benefits for wise investing:

A solid foundation (Matthew 7:24-25) - When you build your financial life on God's principles, it survives life's storms.

A stable future (Isaiah 33:6) - God's wisdom provides security that market investments can't guarantee.

A reverent heart (Proverbs 14:16) - Biblical stewardship develops healthy respect for God.

> **"He who wins souls is wise." The wisest investment is in eternal souls." Proverbs 11:30**

Adoniram Judson's Wise Choice

Judson was one of America's brightest young scholars. He could have had a prestigious career and accumulated significant wealth. Instead, Judson became a missionary to Burma. He lost his wife and children to disease, was imprisoned and tortured, and lived in poverty. But Judson translated the Bible into Burmese, planted churches throughout the country, and saw thousands come to Christ. Even through decades of hardship, Judson maintained hope, declaring: "The prospects are as bright as the promises of God." His wisdom lay in looking beyond present suffering to God's faithful character.

The Compound Interest of Wisdom

Here's what's beautiful about wise investing: it compounds over time.

When you invest in a child's spiritual education, you impact not just that child but everyone they influence.

When you support church planting, you're not just starting one church but potentially dozens of churches.

When you give to missions, you're not just reaching one people group but starting movements that reach multiple generations.

Carlos' Blue-Collar Victory

Carlos works in construction, and his income varies with the seasons. "Some months I make good money, some months work is slow," he said. "I used to think tithing was only for people with steady paychecks."

Carlos learned to give based on percentages, not amounts. "When work is good, I give more. When it's slow, I give less, but I still give. God taught me that faithfulness isn't about the amount, it's about the heart behind it."

"My foreman noticed I was different during the slow season," Carlos said. "Instead of panicking about money, I had peace. He asked me about it, and I got to share the Gospel. Now he comes to church with me."

John Bunyan's Prison Wisdom

John Bunyan was imprisoned for 12 years for preaching without a license. From a worldly perspective, those were 12 wasted years when he could have been earning money and building wealth.

Instead, Bunyan wrote "Pilgrim's Progress" - the most widely read Christian book besides the Bible. His wisdom, gained from prison, has influenced millions of people for over 300 years.

The Wisdom Investment Portfolio

Wise investors diversify their portfolios. Your eternal investment portfolio should include:

Education - Supporting Bible teaching and Christian education

Evangelism - Investing in reaching lost souls with the Gospel

Encouragement - Supporting ministries that strengthen believers

Equipping - Training leaders for kingdom service

Your Wisdom Assessment

Ask yourself these questions:

1. Am I investing for this life only or for eternity?
2. Do my financial decisions reflect God's wisdom or the world's wisdom?
3. What eternal impact will my current spending patterns produce?
4. If I died today, what would my investment portfolio say about my priorities?

The Wisdom Challenge

James 1:5 promises: "If any of you lacks wisdom, let him ask of God, who gives to all liberally and without reproach, and it will be given to him."

This week, before you make any financial decision, ask God for wisdom. Then follow His guidance, even if it doesn't make sense to worldly thinking.

Prayer for Today: *God, I ask that Your wisdom guide my financial decisions, not the world's wisdom. Help me see beyond temporary pleasure to eternal consequences. Give me the wisdom to invest in things that matter forever, not just things that matter today. Make me wise like the five virgins who prepared for a longer wait than expected. Every Christian needs Your wisdom to live victoriously. Amen.*

DAY 21: INVESTING IN THE FUTURE REQUIRES WORK

TODAY'S FOCUS: **The Effort Required for Eternal Impact**

Scripture Reading: 1 Corinthians 15:58

Here's something our culture doesn't want to hear: **Meaningful investment requires meaningful work.**

> **We live in a microwave society that wants instant results. Push a button, get immediate gratification. Swipe a card, get instant credit. Click a link, get instant information.**

But eternal impact doesn't work that way.

The Biblical Work Ethic

God doesn't save you because of your works, but He saves you for good works.

Ephesians 2:10 says: "We are His workmanship, created in Christ Jesus for good works, which God prepared beforehand that we should walk in them."

Notice: God prepared works for you to do. Your eternal investment requires you to do them.

Three Types of Work Investment

1. Your Labor is Required (Ephesians 2:10)

Every believer is enlisted in God's service. This isn't optional - it's why you were saved.

You don't get to sit on the sidelines while others do the work. You don't get to write checks while others serve. God has specific work prepared for you.

2. Your Labor is Recorded (2 Corinthians 5:10)

"We must all appear before the judgment seat of Christ, that each one may receive the things done in the body, according to what he has done, whether good or bad."

God keeps detailed records of:

- Your service for His kingdom
- Your words that encourage or discourage others
- Your small acts of kindness that seem insignificant

> **Nothing you do for Christ is forgotten or wasted.**

3. Your Labor is Rewarded (1 Corinthians 3:11-15)

There will come a day when all believers will have their works tested by fire. Works done with proper motives and methods will survive and be rewarded. Works done for selfish reasons will be burned up.

William Carey's Work Ethic

Carey worked as a cobbler to support his family while teaching himself Latin, Greek, Hebrew, and several other languages.

When Carey felt called to missions, people told him it was impossible. His response: "I can plod. I can persevere in any definite pursuit. To this I owe everything." Carey's "plodding" efforts led to the translation of the Bible into dozens of languages and the establishment of the modern missionary movement.

The Work-Investment Connection

Many Christians want to invest in God's kingdom without doing the work required to make that investment effective. They want to give money to missions without learning about the mission field. They want to support children's ministry without investing time with children. They want to fund church planting without helping plant churches. But effective eternal investment requires personal involvement, not just financial contribution.

Charles Spurgeon's Labor Investment

Charles Spurgeon didn't just preach sermons - he built schools, trained pastors, supported orphanages, and wrote books. Spurgeon said, "By perseverance, the snail reached the ark." He understood that consistent work over time produces greater results than sporadic bursts of activity.

The Labor Multiplication Effect

When you combine work with financial investment, something powerful happens:

You understand what you're investing in - Personal involvement gives you insight into how your money is being used.

You invest more wisely - Experience helps you discern which ministries are effective and which aren't.

You multiply your impact - Your time and money working together accomplish more than either alone.

You experience greater joy - There's satisfaction in seeing the direct results of your labor and investment.

John Newton's Prison Work

Newton could have been bitter about his difficult circumstances as a new Christian. Instead, he worked hard to grow spiritually and help others. Looking back on his journey, Newton gratefully acknowledged: "The Lord has led me about and instructed me and kept me as the apple of His eye." His willingness to work through difficulties led to the writing of "Amazing Grace" and contributed to the eventual end of slavery in England.

The Modern Work Challenge

Our culture promotes a "prosperity gospel" that promises blessings without effort. Just have faith, give generously, and God will provide for you. But the Bible teaches a "productivity gospel" - blessing comes through faithful work in partnership with God.

> **"If anyone will not work, neither shall he eat." 2 Thessalonians 3:10**

Your Work Investment Assessment

Honestly evaluate your eternal work investment:

1. **Time**: How many hours per week do you work for God's kingdom? (Not just attend church, but actively serve)
2. **Energy**: Are you giving your best effort to kingdom work or just your leftovers?
3. **Skills**: Are you using your best abilities for God's purposes or saving them for secular success?
4. **Learning**: Are you growing in knowledge and skill to become more effective in kingdom work?

. . .

The Work Promise

The Apostle Paul gives us a promise in 1 Corinthians 15:58 "Be steadfast, immovable, always abounding in the work of the Lord, knowing that your labor is not in vain in the Lord." Your work for God's kingdom is never wasted. Even when you can't see immediate results, God is using your labor for eternal purposes.

Prayer for Today: *God, help me understand that eternal investment requires personal work, not just financial contribution. Show me the specific work You've prepared for me to do. Give me the discipline to labor faithfully even when I don't see immediate results. Work for the night is coming, when no one can work. Make my labor and my money work together for maximum kingdom impact. Amen.*

DAY 22: INVESTING IN THE FUTURE MEANS WARFARE

TODAY'S FOCUS: **Fighting the Spiritual Battle for Generous Living**

Scripture Reading: Ephesians 6:10-18

You have an enemy who doesn't want you to invest in God's kingdom.

His name is Satan, and he has three primary strategies to keep your money out of God's work:

1. **Convince you that you don't have enough** (fear)
2. **Convince you that you deserve to keep it all** (greed)
3. **Convince you that God doesn't need it** (doubt)

> **Your generous giving is an act of spiritual warfare.**

Know Your Enemy

Satan isn't some mythical creature with horns and a pitchfork. He's a genuine spiritual being with genuine power and a genuine agenda.

He seeks to devour you (1 Peter 5:8) - Like a roaring lion, he looks for Christians who are vulnerable to his financial attacks.

He seeks to deter you (Genesis 3:1) - He questions God's promises about blessing generous givers.

He seeks to deceive you (2 Corinthians 11:14) - He disguises selfishness as wisdom and greed as prudence.

Understand the Battle

Your fight against Satan's financial lies is unlike any earthly conflict:

- **It's spiritual warfare** (Ephesians 6:12) - "We do not wrestle against flesh and blood, but against principalities, against powers, against the rulers of the darkness of this age."
- **It's separated warfare** (2 Timothy 2:4) - As a soldier of Christ, you must disentangle yourself from civilian pursuits that hinder your effectiveness.

- **It requires spiritual armor** (Ephesians 6:11) - You need God's protection to stand against Satan's schemes.

John Bunyan's Warfare Experience

Bunyan was imprisoned for 12 years for preaching the Gospel. During that time, he experienced intense spiritual warfare.

Bunyan wrote: "The enemy so assaulted me with doubts and fears concerning my eternal state, that because of my terror I could not tell what to do." But Bunyan learned to fight back with Scripture and prayer. His writing, inspired by his warfare, led to the creation of "Pilgrim's Progress," which has helped millions of Christians understand spiritual warfare.

Your Financial Armor

Here's how to use God's armor in financial warfare:

- **Belt of Truth** - Know what God says about money and giving, not what culture says.
- **Breastplate of Righteousness** - Live according to God's financial principles, not your feelings.
- **Gospel of Peace** - Remember that generous giving brings peace, not anxiety.
- **Shield of Faith** - Trust God's promises about provision and blessing.
- **Helmet of Salvation** - Remember that your security comes from God, not your bank account.

- **Sword of the Spirit** - Use Scripture to counter Satan's lies about money.

Satan's Three Financial Lies

Lie #1: "You can't afford to give." Truth: "God "will take care of you (2 Corinthians 9:8).

Lie #2: "You earned it, so you deserve to keep it." Truth: What do you have that you didn't receive and that came from above? (James 1:17).

Lie #3: "God doesn't need your money." Truth: "God is not served by human hands, as if he needed anything" - but He wants your heart, and your money reveals your heart (Acts 17:25; Matthew 6:21).

George Whitefield's Warfare Victory

George Whitefield faced constant spiritual warfare as he preached to massive crowds across America and England. Satan attacked him with pride, discouragement, and financial temptation. But Whitefield learned to fight back through generous giving and radical faith. He understood his calling with eternal perspective, declaring: "We are immortal until our work on earth is done." This confidence in God's sovereignty enabled him to take risks with his finances and ministry that others considered foolish.

The Three Expectations That Keep You Fighting

1. The expectation of His return (Titus 2:13) - Jesus is coming back, and you want to be found faithful when He arrives.

2. The expectation of His reward (Revelation 22:12) - Christ will bring rewards with Him for faithful stewards.

3. The expectation of His redemption (Ephesians 1:14) - Your body will be redeemed, and your faithful investment will be complete.

Your Financial Battle Plan

Here's how to fight the good fight with your money:

- **Daily**: Put on God's armor through prayer and Scripture reading before making any financial decisions.
- **Weekly**: Evaluate your spending to see if you're winning or losing the spiritual battle.
- **Monthly**: Give Satan a defeat by making a sacrificial gift to God's kingdom.
- **Yearly**: Review your financial warfare - are you more generous now than you were 12 months ago?

The Victory Promise

In 1 John 4:4, we read and are reminded: "He who is in you is greater than he who is in the world." Satan is powerful, but God is more powerful. Satan has schemes, but God has promises. Satan wants to steal your joy through financial fear, but God wants to give you peace through financial faithfulness.

William Carey's Warfare Wisdom

Carey also faced enormous spiritual warfare as he pioneered missions to India. Satan attacked through discouragement, opposition, and financial pressure. But Carey kept fighting by continuing to give generously even when he had little. He said, "The future is as bright as the promises of God."

Prayer for Today: *God, help me recognize that my financial decisions are a form of spiritual warfare. Give me the strength to fight against Satan's lies with Your truth. Protect me from fear, greed, and doubt. Help me use my money as a weapon against the enemy's kingdom and a tool for Your kingdom. Thank You that I can have victory in this battle through Jesus Christ. Amen.*

DAY 23: INVESTING IN THE FUTURE BRINGS WEALTH

TODAY'S FOCUS: **Understanding True Riches That Last Forever**

Scripture Reading: 1 Timothy 6:17-19

What if I told you that you could become wealthy beyond your wildest dreams, but it would require giving away most of what you currently own? You'd probably think I was crazy.

But that's precisely what Jesus taught.

"Sell what you have and give alms; provide yourselves money bags which do not grow old, a treasure in the heavens that does not fail" (Luke 12:33).

The Three Types of Wealth

1. Temporal Riches (What Most People Pursue)

These are the riches you can see, touch, and count:

- Money in the bank
- Houses and cars
- Investments and possessions
- Anything that has a price tag

The problem with temporal riches: They don't last on earth, so that is why we can not set our mind on it while on earth.

"Set your mind on things above, not on things on the earth." Colossians 3:2

> **God isn't opposed to temporal riches. He's against trusting in them.**

Paul says: "Command those who are rich in this present age not to be haughty, nor to trust in uncertain riches but in the living God" (1 Timothy 6:17).

2. True Riches (What Smart People Pursue)

Jesus talked about "true riches" that are different from temporal riches:

1. **True wealth doesn't lie in the abundance of possessions** (Luke 12:15) - Your life's value isn't measured by what you own.

2. **True wealth doesn't lie in laying up treasure for yourself** (Luke 12:21) - Selfish accumulation isn't wealth; it's spiritual poverty.
3. **True wealth lies in seeking God's kingdom** (Matthew 6:33) - When you prioritize God's purposes, He takes care of your needs.

3. Timeless Riches (What Wise People Pursue)
These are riches that last forever:

1. **God's great investment** (John 3:16) - God gave His only Son for your salvation. That's the most significant investment in history.
2. **God's great invitation** (Isaiah 1:18) - Though your sins are like scarlet, God offers to make them white as snow.
3. **Your great impact** (Mark 8:36) - What does it profit if you gain the whole world but lose your soul? The souls you influence for Christ are timeless riches.

John Newton's Wealth Transformation

Newton was a slave trader who pursued temporal riches through human trafficking. He accumulated significant wealth but was spiritually bankrupt. When Newton came to Christ, his understanding of wealth underwent a complete transformation. He gave up the slave trade, became a pastor, and spent his income helping others find freedom in Christ. Newton wrote: "Amazing grace, how sweet the sound, that saved a wretch like me." Newton discovered that spiritual wealth far exceeded financial wealth.

The Wealth Exchange Program

Here's how God's wealth exchange program works:

You give: Temporal riches (money, possessions, comfort)
You get: Timeless riches (relationships, purpose, eternal treasure)

You invest: In things that decay.
You receive: Things that last forever.

You sacrifice: Temporary pleasure.
You gain: Permanent joy

Betty's Elderly Encouragement

Betty lives on Social Security and a small pension. "After my husband died, I thought my giving days were over," she said. "The financial advisor told me to hoard every penny."

But Betty remembered the widow's mites story and decided to keep giving her $10 weekly offering. "I may not have much money, but I have time," she said. Betty volunteers 20 hours a week at her church.

"I discovered that giving isn't just about money - it's about giving your life," Betty said. "I may be poor in this world's eyes, but I'm rich in the ways that matter to God."

Charles Spurgeon's Wealth Philosophy

Spurgeon could have been wealthy by any measure. He pastored the largest church in the world, wrote bestselling books, and was offered huge sums to tour America. Instead, Spurgeon gave away most of his income. He said: "It is not how much we have, but how much we enjoy, that makes happiness." Spurgeon died with little money but enormous influence. His sermons are still read worldwide 150 years later.

The Compound Interest of Generosity

When you invest in God's kingdom, something amazing happens: your investment compounds eternally. The person you help lead to Christ may, in turn, lead others to Christ. The church you support may plant other churches. The missionary you fund may start a movement that lasts for generations.

Adoniram Judson's Eternal Investment

Judson gave up a promising career in America to be a missionary to Burma. By worldly standards, he had lost everything: wealth, comfort, family, and health.

But Judson's investment in Burma led to:

- Thousands of people finding Christ
- The entire Bible translated into Burmese
- Churches planted throughout the country
- A Christian movement that continues today

On his deathbed, Judson said: "I am not tired of my work, neither am I tired of the world; yet when Christ calls me home, I shall go with the gladness of a boy bounding away from school."

The Wealth Assessment

Ask yourself these questions:

1. What type of wealth am I primarily pursuing?

2. If I lost all my temporal riches tomorrow, what true riches would I still have?

3. What timeless riches am I building through my current investments?

4. When I die, what type of wealth will people say I accumulated?

The Rich Young Ruler's Choice

Jesus once met a wealthy young man who asked how to inherit eternal life. Jesus told him, "Sell all that you have and distribute to the poor, and you will have treasure in heaven; and come, follow Me" (Luke 18:22). The man walked away sad because he loved his temporal riches more than timeless riches.

That same choice is before you every day.

Your Wealth Investment Strategy

Here's how to build authentic and timeless wealth:

Daily: Make financial decisions based on eternal values, not temporary desires.
Weekly: Give something away that has real value to you.
Monthly: Evaluate whether your spending builds temporal or timeless wealth.
Yearly: Increase your investment in God's kingdom as He increases your resources.

The Wealth Promise

Jesus promised: "Everyone who has left houses or brothers or sisters or father or mother or wife or children or lands, for My name's sake, shall receive a hundredfold, and inherit eternal life" (Matthew 19:29). That's not just a promise for missionaries and pastors. That's a promise for anyone who invests in God's kingdom, rather than just their own.

Prayer for Today: *God, help me understand the difference between temporal riches, true riches, and timeless riches. Give me wisdom to pursue the wealth that matters forever, not just the wealth that matters today. Transform my definition of success from accumulation to generosity. The souls we invest in are of eternal value! Use my resources to build Your kingdom and store up treasure in heaven. Amen.*

DAY 24: REVIEW AND ETERNAL PERSPECTIVE

TODAY'S FOCUS: **Completing Your Investment in Eternity**

This week, we've focused on the eternal implications of your financial choices. Let's review and prepare for a lifetime of wise kingdom investment.

Week 4 Key Principles:

1. **Avoiding Wrath** - Your money choices reveal your relationship with God and impact your eternal destiny.
2. **Gaining Wisdom** - God's financial wisdom leads to eternal security, while worldly wisdom leads to temporal success at best.
3. **Working Faithfully** - Effective eternal investment requires personal labor, not just financial contribution.

4. Fighting Spiritually - Your generous giving is spiritual warfare against Satan's kingdom of greed and fear.

5. Building True Wealth - Timeless riches matter more than temporal riches, and true wealth comes through generous investment in God's kingdom.

The Complete Investment Journey

Over four weeks, we've traveled from foundational principles to eternal perspective:

Week 1: God's investment principles (Submission, Servanthood, Sowing/Reaping, Sacrifice, Steadfastness)
Week 2: Life transformation stages (Crucified, Victorious, Spirit-Filled, Fruitful, Abundant)
Week 3: Church investment practices (Honor, Trust, Give, Testify, Thank)
Week 4: Eternal perspective motivation (Avoid Wrath, Gain Wisdom, Work Faithfully, Fight Spiritually, Build True Wealth)

Charles Spurgeon's Complete Vision

Spurgeon understood the complete investment journey. He said, "A good character is the best tombstone. Those who loved you and were helped by you will remember you when forget-me-nots have withered. Carve your name on hearts, not on marble." Spurgeon invested his money in carving his name on hearts through Gospel ministry. His temporal investments are forgotten, but his eternal investments continue producing fruit 150 years later.

Your Investment Legacy

What legacy will your financial choices leave?

Temporal Legacy: The money you accumulate, the possessions you acquire, the comfort you create - all of which stays behind when you die.

Eternal Legacy: The lives you touch, the souls you reach, the kingdom you advance - all of which follows you into eternity.

The Final Assessment

Before we conclude this journey, honestly assess where you are:

Foundation: Have I surrendered my finances to God's principles? (Week 1)
Transformation: Am I progressing through the stages of spiritual maturity? (Week 2)
Investment: Am I faithfully investing in the local church? (Week 3)
Perspective: Do I make financial decisions with eternity in mind? (Week 4)

John Newton's Complete Transformation

Newton's journey illustrates the complete investment transformation:

Foundation: He submitted his life and finances to God after his conversion.

Transformation: He progressed from slave trader to pastor, growing in spiritual maturity.
Investment: He invested heavily in his local church and theological education.
Perspective: He made every financial decision with eternity in mind, giving away most of his income.

The result? Newton's investment in God's kingdom helped bring about the abolition of slavery in the British Empire and continues to inspire people worldwide through "Amazing Grace."

Your Investment Commitment

I want you to think about what specific commitments you will make.

Daily: How will you apply God's investment principles in everyday financial decisions?
Weekly: What regular giving pattern will you establish?
Monthly: How will you evaluate and adjust your kingdom investment?
Yearly: How will you increase your investment as God blesses you?

The 50-Year Question

Here's a question to put everything in perspective:

50 years from now, what will matter most about how you handled money this year?

Will it matter that you had a nice car? Probably not. Will it matter that you lived in a beautiful house? Probably not. Will it matter that you had a large retirement account? Probably not.

But it will matter enormously if:

• You helped support a missionary who reached an unreached people group

• You gave to a church that planted other churches

• You supported a ministry that led your neighbor to Christ

• You invested in a child's education who became a pastor

William Carey's 50-Year Impact

William Carey died in 1834. He had little money and few possessions.

But 50 years later, the impact of his financial investments in missions was staggering:

• The Bible had been translated into hundreds of languages

• Churches had been planted on every continent

• The modern missionary movement was reaching millions

Carey chose eternal impact over temporal accumulation. His investment strategy is still paying dividends 200 years later.

Your Eternal Investment

Paul told Timothy, "For we brought nothing into this world, and it is certain we can carry nothing out." (1 Timothy 6:7). Invest where it matters.

Your money follows your heart, but your heart also follows your money. When you invest in God's kingdom, your heart becomes more attached to God's purposes.

Prayer for Today: *God, thank You for this journey of learning Your heart for investment and generosity. Help me apply these principles for the rest of my life. Give me wisdom to make every financial decision with eternity in mind. Use my investments to advance Your kingdom and bring glory to Your name. Help me finish strong in faithful stewardship. Amen.*

CHAPTER 5
WEEK FIVE: INVESTING FOR LEGACY

> **Memory Verse:** *A good man leaves an inheritance to his children's children, but the wealth of the sinner is stored up for the righteous."* Proverbs 13:22

DAY 25: YOUR ETERNITY INVESTMENT ACTION PLAN

TODAY'S FOCUS: **Turning Knowledge into Practice**

Scripture Reading: James 1:22-25

James wrote: "Be doers of the word, and not hearers only, deceiving yourselves" (James 1:22).

You've spent many days learning God's principles for biblical investment. Now it's time to put them into practice.

Knowledge without action is worthless.

The Danger of Information Without Implementation

Jesus told a story about two builders. One heard His words and acted on them - his house survived the storm. The other listened to His words but didn't act on them - his house collapsed (Matthew 7:24-27).

The difference wasn't in what they heard. The difference was in what they did with what they heard.

Your Investment Action Plan

Here's a practical framework for implementing what you've learned:

Step 1: Assess Your Current Reality

Before you can change direction, you need to know where you are. Honestly evaluate:

Your Foundation (Week 1 Principles):

- Am I submitted to God's financial plan or my own?
- Do I see myself as God's steward or money's owner?
- Am I sowing for eternity or just for time?
- Does my giving cost me something, or is it just convenient?
- Am I consistent in my giving or just emotional?

Your Transformation (Week 2 Stages):

- Have I died to selfish financial desires (Crucified Life)?
- Am I overcoming the enemies of generous living (Victorious Life)?
- Do I let the Holy Spirit guide my money decisions (Spirit-Filled Life)?
- Is my money producing eternal fruit (Fruitful Life)?
- Am I experiencing joy through generosity (Abundant Life)?

Your Investment (Week 3 Practices):

- Do I honor my church's divine purpose?
- Do I trust God to work through my church?
- Am I giving my time, treasure, and talents?
- Is my testimony connected to my church community?
- Do I express gratitude for my church's ministry?

Your Perspective (Week 4 Motivation):

- Are my financial choices helping people escape God's wrath?
- Do I make decisions based on God's wisdom or worldly wisdom?
- Am I working faithfully for God's kingdom?
- Do I recognize financial decisions as spiritual warfare?
- Am I building temporal or timeless wealth?

Step 2: Identify Your Next Steps

You can't change everything at once, but you can make a change right now. Based on your assessment, what are your top three areas for growth?

Example priorities:

1. "I need to start giving consistently instead of just when I feel like it."
2. "I need to get involved in serving at my church, not just attending."
3. "I need to seek the Holy Spirit's guidance before making financial decisions."

Step 3: Make Specific Commitments

Vague goals produce vague results. Specific commitments produce specific changes.

- **Instead of**: "I want to give more."
- **Commit to**: "I will give $X every month for the next six months."
- **Instead of**: "I should serve at church."
- **Commit to**: "I will volunteer for X ministry starting this Sunday."
- **Instead of**: "I need to be more spiritual with money."
- **Commit to**: "I will pray before every purchase over $X."

Charles Spurgeon's Action Approach

Charles Spurgeon didn't just preach about generous living - he practiced it. He said, "The Bible was not given for our information but for our transformation." Spurgeon established specific systems for giving:

- A set percentage of his income went to church ministries
    - A portion supported theological education
    - Regular amounts went to help the poor
    - Special offerings funded missions and church planting

Step 4: Create Accountability

Change is hard. You need accountability to stay committed to your investment action plan.

- **Find an accountability partner** - someone who will ask you regularly about your financial commitments.
- **Track your progress** - keep records of your giving, serving, and spiritual growth.
- **Celebrate victories** - acknowledge when you successfully apply biblical principles.
- **Learn from failures** - when you fail (and you will), learn from it and get back on track.

Step 5: Plan for Growth

Your investment action plan should include growth over time.

John Newton's Growth Pattern

Newton began his Christian journey in small ways. He couldn't immediately give large amounts or serve in significant ways. But Newton established a pattern of growth:

- Year 1: Basic giving and church attendance
- Year 2: Increased giving and began serving
- Year 3: Sacrificial giving and teaching others
- Years 4+: Major ministry investment and leadership

Newton's action plan led to a lifetime of kingdom impact.

Your 90-Day Quick Start

Here's a simple 90-day plan to begin implementing what you've learned:

- **Days 1-30**: Establish consistent giving (even if it's small) and regular church attendance.
- **Days 31-60**: Add service to your routine - volunteer for one church ministry.
- **Days 61-90**: Increase your giving amount or percentage, and invite someone to join you in church.

The Action Promise

Jesus promised: "If you know these things, blessed are you if you do them" (John 13:17).

> **The blessing doesn't come from knowing God's principles. The blessing comes from doing God's principles.**

Your Action Commitment

Complete these statements:

"This week, I will begin

____"

"This month, I will establish

____"

"This year, I will increase

____"

"For the rest of my life, I will commit to

____"

Prayer for Today: *God, help me be a doer of Your Word, not just a hearer. Please give me courage to take specific action on what I've learned. Help me start where I am, use what I have, and do what I can. Make my action plan a blessing to Your kingdom and a source of joy in my life. Transform my knowledge into practice. Amen.*

DAY 26: BUILDING YOUR SUPPORT SYSTEM

TODAY'S FOCUS: **Creating Community for Faithful Stewardship**

Scripture Reading: Ecclesiastes 4:9-12

"Two are better than one, because they have a good return for their labor. If either of them falls down, one can help the other up" (Ecclesiastes 4:9-10).

> **Faithful stewardship is easier with loyal friends.**

The Isolation Trap

Our culture promotes financial independence - the idea that you should make your own money decisions. But God designed us for community, especially when it comes to important life decisions.

When you try to live generously in isolation, several things happen:

- You lack encouragement when giving feels difficult
- You miss wisdom from others who've faced similar challenges
- You have no accountability for your commitments
- You don't see examples of faithful stewardship in action

Biblical Community Models

The Early Church (Acts 2:42-47) - They shared everything in common, supporting each other's needs and encouraging generous living.
Paul's Ministry Teams (multiple books) - Paul always traveled with companions who shared his vision and supported his ministry financially and emotionally.
Jesus' Disciples (Luke 8:1-3) - Even Jesus had a support system of people who funded His ministry and traveled with Him.

Charles Spurgeon's Community
Charles Spurgeon surrounded himself with like-minded people who shared his commitment to generous living:

- **Deacons** who helped him identify needs and opportunities for giving
- **Fellow pastors** who encouraged his sacrificial lifestyle
- **Wealthy members** who joined him in significant ministry investments

- **Poor members** who inspired him through their sacrificial giving

Spurgeon said, "A man wrapped up in himself makes a very small bundle."

Building Your Stewardship Support System

1. Find a Financial Accountability Partner

This should be someone who:

- Shares your commitment to biblical stewardship
- Has permission to ask you hard questions about money
- Will encourage you when generosity feels difficult
- Models faithful stewardship in their own lives

Meet monthly to discuss:

- How you're applying biblical financial principles
- Specific giving and serving commitments
- Challenges you're facing with money decisions
- Opportunities you see for kingdom investment

2. Join a Small Group or Bible Study

Find a group that:

- Studies biblical financial principles together

- Prays for each other's stewardship decisions
- Shares testimonies of God's faithfulness in provision
- Plans group service projects and giving opportunities

3. Connect with Generous Mentors

Look for people who:

- Have been faithfully generous for many years
- Can share wisdom from their stewardship journey
- Model joyful giving instead of grudging obligation
- Can help you see opportunities you might miss

John Newton's Mentoring Network

Newton built relationships with both mentors and mentees:

- **Mentors** like George Whitefield taught him about generous living.
- **Peers** like William Cowper encouraged him through difficult times.
- **Mentees** like William Wilberforce learned stewardship principles from him.

This network helped Newton maintain a life of generosity for over 40 years of ministry.

4. Engage Your Family

If you're married or have children, include them in your stewardship journey:

With your spouse:

- Pray together about giving decisions
- Study biblical financial principles together
- Set giving goals together
- Celebrate the kingdom impact together

With your children:

- Let them see you giving generously
- Explain why you make certain financial choices
- Include them in choosing charities to support
- Teach them to give from their own allowance or earnings

William Carey's Family Investment

Carey included his entire family in his commitment to missions. Despite incredible hardships, his family shared his vision for reaching people with the Gospel. William's son became a missionary. His family's shared commitment multiplied their kingdom's impact for generations.

5. Find Your Church Community

Your local church should be the center of your stewardship support system:

- **Learn** from teaching about biblical stewardship
- **Give** through church ministries and missions
- **Serve** alongside other committed believers

- **Pray** with others about financial decisions
- **Celebrate** stories of God's faithfulness in provision

Overcoming Community Challenges

"I don't want people knowing my financial business." You don't have to share specific amounts, but you can share principles and struggles.

"Everyone I know is materialistic." Start with one person. Ask God to help you find at least one like-minded friend.

"My spouse isn't interested in biblical stewardship." Begin with your own faithfulness. Let your example, not your words, do the convincing.

"My church doesn't teach about money." Find additional resources and communities outside your church, or respectfully encourage your church to address stewardship.

The Community Promise

Hebrews 10:24-25 says: "Let us consider one another in order to stir up love and good works, not forsaking the assembling of ourselves together ... but exhorting one another."
God designed community to "stir up" good works - including generous giving. When you surround yourself with people who share your values, generous living becomes natural rather than a challenge.

Adoniram Judson's Support System

Judson survived 40 years of missionary service because of his support system:

- A mission board that funded his work
- Fellow missionaries who shared his burdens
- Supporters in America who prayed and gave
- Converts in Burma who encouraged his ministry

Without this community, Judson would never have been able to sustain his sacrificial lifestyle.

Your Community Action Steps

This week, take one concrete step toward building your stewardship support system:

- **Identify** one person who could be a financial accountability partner
- **Research** small groups or Bible studies that focus on biblical stewardship
- **Reach out** to someone whose generous lifestyle you admire
- **Plan** a family conversation about your stewardship goals
- **Get involved** in one new ministry or service opportunity at church

Prayer for Today: *God, help me build a community that supports faithful stewardship. Bring people into my life who share my commitment to a generous way of living. Please help me be an encourager to others who want to live biblically with money. Use our community to stir up love and good works that advance Your kingdom. Don't let me try to do this alone. Amen.*

DAY 27: HANDLING SETBACKS AND FAILURES

TODAY'S FOCUS: **Getting Back on Track When You Fall Short**

Scripture Reading: 1 John 1:8-10

Let me be honest with you: **You're going to fail at faithful stewardship sometimes.**

You'll have months when you don't give what you planned to give. You'll make purchases you regret. You'll choose selfishness over generosity. You'll let fear override faith.

. . .

The question isn't whether you'll fail; the question is whether you'll succeed. The question is what you'll do when you fail.

The Reality of Spiritual Failure

John wrote: "If we say that we have no sin, we deceive ourselves, and the truth is not in us" (1 John 1:8).

This includes financial sin:

- Greed that chooses accumulation over generosity
- Fear that hoards instead of trusts
- Pride that gives recognition instead of love
- Selfishness that ignores others' needs

Even mature Christians struggle with money issues.

Biblical Examples of Financial Failure

- **David**, despite being "a man after God's own heart," failed morally and financially later in life due to pride and poor decisions.
- **Solomon**, the wisest man who ever lived, ended up accumulating enormous wealth for selfish purposes rather than God's glory.
- **The Rich Young Ruler** - A moral, religious person who loved money more than Jesus.
- **Ananias and Sapphira** - church members who lied about their giving to appear more generous than they were.

John Newton's Failure and Recovery

Newton's journey wasn't one of instant perfection. Even after his dramatic conversion, he continued to wrestle with the temptation to make selfish financial decisions. But Newton learned to trust God's grace through every failure. Near the end of his life, despite failing memory, he declared: "My memory is nearly gone, but I remember two things: That I am a great sinner, and that Christ is a great Savior." This grace-centered perspective helped Newton maintain hope during his own setbacks and failures in stewardship.

Common Stewardship Failures

1. **Consistency Failure**: You commit to giving regularly but skip months when money is tight.
2. **Generosity Failure**: You give grudgingly instead of cheerfully, or you give less than you know you should.
3. **Priority Failure**: You spend money on wants while ignoring important kingdom needs.
4. **Trust Failure**: You hoard money out of fear instead of trusting God's provision.
5. **Wisdom Failure**: You make financial decisions without seeking God's guidance.

How to Respond to Financial Failure

1. Acknowledge the Failure Honestly

Don't minimize it: "It's not that bad." Don't justify it: "I had a good reason." Don't blame others: "My spouse made me do it."

1 John 1:9 promises: "If we confess our sins, He is faithful and just to forgive us our sins and to cleanse us from all unrighteousness."

2. Learn from the Failure

Ask yourself:

• What led to this failure? (circumstances, emotions, poor planning)
• What lies did I believe? (fear, greed, pride)
• What truth do I need to remember? (God's promises, biblical principles)
• How can I prevent this failure in the future? (accountability, boundaries, better systems)

3. Make Specific Changes

Don't just say: "I'll do better next time." Instead, decide: "I will do X differently to prevent this from happening again."

Examples:

• Set up automatic giving so you can't skip months
• Find an accountability partner to help with major purchases
• Establish a giving budget that you follow regardless of emotions
• Create margins in your budget so you're not constantly stressed about money

Charles Spurgeon's Recovery Wisdom

Spurgeon said, "I have learned to kiss the wave that throws me against the Rock of Ages." Spurgeon recognized that even painful trials and setbacks can drive us closer to Christ. In seasons of personal financial struggle or spiritual relapse, he didn't waste his suffering; he used it as momentum to return to the Lord. Recovery for Spurgeon wasn't about avoiding hardship but learning to find God in the midst of it and keep moving forward.

4. Get Back on Track Immediately

The longer you wait to resume faithful stewardship, the harder it becomes.

Don't think: "I'll start fresh next month." Instead, think: "I'll start fresh right now."

If you missed giving last month, give this month. If you made a selfish purchase yesterday, make a generous gift today. If you've been hoarding out of fear, take a step of faith this week.

5. Focus on Progress, Not Perfection

Carey faced enormous spiritual warfare as he pioneered missions to India. Satan attacked through discouragement, opposition, and financial pressure. But Carey understood the importance of community support in overcoming failure. When facing criticism about his mission plans, Carey famously said: "I will go down, if you will hold the rope." He knew that faithful service requires both personal courage and community support, especially when recovering from setbacks.

The Grace Factor

Here's the good news:

> **God's grace is bigger than your stewardship failures.**

Jesus didn't die for perfect people. He died for people who struggle with sin, including financial sin.

Your identity isn't "failed steward." Your identity is "beloved child of God who is learning to be generous."

Adoniram Judson's Perseverance

Judson faced repeated failures and setbacks during 40 years of missionary service:

- Financial supporters withdrew their support
- Fellow missionaries died or returned home
- Government officials opposed his ministry
- Personal tragedies tested his faith

But Judson said: "I never was deeply interested in any object, I never prayed sincerely and earnestly for anything, but it came at some time."

Judson's perseverance in the face of failure led to a lasting impact on the kingdom.

Your Failure Recovery Plan

When you fail at faithful stewardship:

Step 1: Confess the failure to God and receive His forgiveness.

Step 2: Identify what led to the failure and what you can learn from it.

Step 3: Implement specific changes to prevent the same failure from occurring in the future.

Step 4: Get back on track immediately - don't wait for a "fresh start."

Step 5: Focus on your next faithful choice, not your last unfaithful choice.

The Comeback Promise

Micah 7:8 says: "Do not rejoice over me, my enemy; when I fall, I will arise; when I sit in darkness, the Lord will be a light to me."

> **Your stewardship failures don't have to define you. God's grace is sufficient to lift you and get you back on track.**

Prayer for Today: *God, thank You that Your grace is bigger than my stewardship failures. Help me respond to failure with humility, learning, and quick obedience. Don't let me be discouraged by my mistakes or take pride in my successes. Keep me focused on growth, not perfection. When I fall, please help me get back up quickly and keep moving forward in a life of generosity. Amen.*

DAY 28: YOUR LIFELONG INVESTMENT LEGACY

TODAY'S FOCUS: **Finishing Strong in Faithful Stewardship**

Scripture Reading: 2 Timothy 4:6-8

Paul wrote near the end of his life: "I have fought the good fight, I have finished the race, I have kept the faith. Finally, there is laid up for me the crown of righteousness" (2 Timothy 4:7-8).

Today, we reflect on how you would like to conclude your stewardship journey.

The Legacy Question

Imagine you're 90 years old, looking back on your life. What do you want people to say about how you handled money?

"He accumulated a lot of wealth." "She lived very comfortably." "They had nice things."

Or:

"He was incredibly generous." "She invested in God's kingdom." "They used their resources to change lives."

> **Your financial legacy isn't determined by how much you accumulate; it's determined by how you manage it. It's defined by how much you invest in eternity.**

Three Types of Legacy

1. The Accumulation Legacy

This person's obituary reads: "He was successful in business and accumulated significant wealth. He provided well for his family and enjoyed the finer things in life."

The problem: This legacy comes to an end with death. Within a generation or two, most people will likely forget what you have accumulated.

2. The Contribution Legacy

This person's obituary reads: "She was known for her generous heart and faithful service. She supported many good causes and helped countless people in need."

Better, but limited: This legacy impacts this life but may not extend into eternity.

3. The Kingdom Legacy

This person's obituary reads: "His life was invested in advancing God's kingdom. Churches were planted, missionaries were supported, souls were reached, and lives were transformed through his faithful stewardship."

The eternal impact: This legacy endures forever through the people it reaches and the ministries it supports.

John Newton's Kingdom Legacy

Newton died in 1807 with little money in the bank. But his kingdom legacy includes:

- "Amazing Grace" - sung by millions for over 200 years
- The abolitionist movement, which he helped inspire through his testimony
- Countless pastors, who were trained through ministries he supported
- Churches planted, using principles he taught about generous living

Newton chose kingdom legacy over accumulation legacy, and his influence continues 200+ years later.

Charles Spurgeon's Multiplication Legacy

Spurgeon could have lived luxuriously as the most famous preacher of his day. Instead, he invested almost everything in kingdom work:

- The Pastor's College, which trained thousands of ministers
- Orphanages, which cared for hundreds of children
- Mission work, which planted churches around the world
- Publishing ministry, which continues to influence people today

Spurgeon said, "A good character is the best tombstone. Those who loved you and were helped by you will remember you when forget-me-nots have withered."

Building Your Kingdom Legacy

Start with the End in Mind

Business leader Stephen Covey taught people to "begin with the end in mind." What kind of stewardship legacy do you want to leave?

Write your obituary focusing on stewardship: "He/She was known for ..."

Think Generationally

Your legacy will impact multiple generations:

- **Your children** learn generosity by watching you
- **Your grandchildren** inherit your values along with your resources
- **Your church** continues the ministries you supported
- **Missions** you funded may reach people for generations

William Carey's Generational Impact

Carey's investment in missions had a lasting impact on his generation. The Bible translations, churches, and educational institutions he established in India continue impacting people 200 years later.

Carey's son became a missionary. His disciples became missionaries. The movement he started continues today.

Adoniram Judson's Enduring Legacy

Judson spent 40 years in Burma (Myanmar), investing his life and resources in reaching the Burmese people despite incredible hardships. Near the end of his life, Judson reflected with profound wisdom: "A life once spent is irrevocable. It will remain to be contemplated through eternity." This eternal perspective shaped his complete devotion, producing joy that came from knowing his investment had eternal value - transforming an entire nation through the Gospel.

Your Legacy Investment Strategy

1. Invest in People, Not Just Programs

Programs end. People are eternal. Focus your stewardship on investments that develop people:

- Supporting missionaries who will train national leaders
- Funding education that builds character along with skills
- Investing in church planting that develops local leadership

2. Think Multiplication, Not Just Addition

Instead of asking: "How many people can I help?" Ask: "How can I help people who will help people?"

Your investment in training one pastor may reach thousands of people. Your support for one missionary may result in churches that plant other churches. Your investment in one child's education may produce a leader who impacts nations.

3. Combine Immediate Impact with Long-Term Investment

Balance meeting current needs with building for the future:

- Support feeding programs AND agricultural training
- Fund disaster relief AND church planting
- Help with immediate needs AND leadership development

4. Document Your Stewardship Story

Keep records of:

- Why do you make certain stewardship decisions
- Stories of how God has used your investments
- Lessons you've learned about generous living
- Advice you'd give to future generations

Share these stories with your family so they understand the values behind your financial choices.

Your 50-Year Vision

50 years from now:

- What ministries will still exist because of your investment?
- What people will be in heaven because of your stewardship?
- What churches will be thriving because of your support?

• What children will know Christ because of your generosity?

The Legacy Promise

Proverbs 13:22 says: "A good man leaves an inheritance to his children's children."
This isn't just talking about money. It's talking about values, character, and spiritual legacy.

When you live generously, you leave your children and grandchildren an inheritance of:

• Faith in God's provision
• Joy in generous living
• Purpose of the kingdom investment
• Hope in eternal rewards

John Bunyan's Prison Legacy

Bunyan was imprisoned for 12 years for preaching without a license. He could have seen this as wasted time when he should have been earning money for his family.

Instead, Bunyan used his prison time to write "Pilgrim's Progress," which has sold more copies than any book except the Bible.
Bunyan's willingness to sacrifice immediate financial security for the long-term impact on the kingdom created a legacy that has influenced millions of people for over 300 years.

Your Legacy Commitment

Complete these statements:

"I want to be remembered as someone who ...

____"

"50 years from now, I want my investments to have

____"

"The values I want to pass to future generations are

____"

"The kingdom impact I want my life to produce is

____"

The Finishing Strong Promise

2 Chronicles 16:9 says: "The eyes of the Lord run to and fro throughout the whole earth, to show Himself strong on behalf of those whose heart is loyal to Him."

God is seeking individuals who will finish strong in faithful stewardship. He wants to show His strength through your generous living.

> **Your stewardship legacy starts today with your next financial decision.**

Prayer for Today: *God, help me build a lasting kingdom legacy. Give me wisdom to invest in people and ministries that will multiply Your kingdom for generations. Help me finish strong in faithful stewardship, not accumulating treasures on earth but laying up treasures in heaven. Use my life and my resources to advance Your kingdom and bring glory to Your name for eternity. Amen.*

CONCLUSION: YOUR FOREVER INVESTMENT BEGINS NOW

Many days ago, you began a journey.

YOU'VE LEARNED God's principles for biblical investment. You've discovered the stages of spiritual growth. You've explored how to invest in the local church. You've gained an eternal perspective on your financial choices.

But here's the truth: Your real journey is just beginning.

The Knowledge-to-Action Bridge

James 1:22 warns: "Be doers of the word, and not hearers only, deceiving yourselves." Everything you've learned over the past 28 days is worthless unless you act on it. The question isn't whether you understand God's principles for money. The question is whether you'll live them.

Your Investment Decision Tree

Every financial decision you make from now on is an opportunity to apply what you've learned. Here's a simple decision tree:

Before every financial choice, ask:

1. Does this honor God or honor myself?
2. Does this advance God's kingdom or my kingdom?
3. Does this reflect eternal values or temporal values?
4. Would Jesus make this choice with His money?

Charles Spurgeon's Final Challenge

Spurgeon said near the end of his life: "I would rather be the means of saving one soul than of preaching to countless multitudes with no result." Spurgeon understood that kingdom impact matters more than personal success.

> **Your money can be the means of saving souls, planting churches, training leaders, and advancing God's kingdom - if you choose to use it that way.**

The Eternal Perspective

100 years from now:

- Strangers will occupy your house
- Your car will be in a junkyard
- Your bank account will belong to someone else
- Your possessions will be forgotten

But:

- The souls reached through your generosity will be in heaven
- The churches planted with your support will still be ministering
- The leaders trained through your investment will still be serving
- The kingdom impact of your stewardship will still be multiplying

John Newton's Final Words

Newton's gravestone reads: "John Newton, clerk, once an infidel and libertine, a servant of slaves in Africa, was, by the rich mercy of our Lord and Savior Jesus Christ, preserved, restored, pardoned, and appointed to preach the faith he had long labored to destroy." Newton wanted to be remembered not for what he accumulated, but for how God's grace transformed him from a selfish slave trader into a generous servant.

Your Stewardship Epitaph

How do you want to be remembered? What do you want written on your gravestone?

"Accumulated great wealth." Or "Invested in great eternity."

The Choice Is Yours

You can choose to live like the rich fool in Jesus' story - accumulating treasures that can't follow you to eternity. You can choose to live like the heroes of faith - investing in treasures that last forever. You can choose to use your money for your kingdom. Or you can choose to use your money for God's kingdom. You can choose to be an owner. Or you can choose to be a steward. You can choose temporal riches. Or you can choose eternal riches.

The Investment Opportunity of a Lifetime

God has great things planned for your stewardship if you'll attempt great things for His kingdom. Your money - whether it's $50 or $50,000 - can be part of the most significant investment opportunity in history: advancing God's kingdom on earth.

The Forever Promise

Jesus promised: "And everyone who has left houses or brothers or sisters or father or mother or wife or children or lands, for My name's sake, shall receive a hundredfold, and inherit eternal life" (Matthew 19:29).

That's not just a promise for missionaries. That's a promise for every believer who chooses to invest in the kingdom over personal accumulation.

Your Forever Investment Starts Now

Don't wait for tomorrow. Don't wait for more money. Don't wait for perfect conditions. Your forever investment begins with your next financial decision. Make it count for eternity.

Final Prayer: *God, thank You for these 28 days of learning Your heart for stewardship and generosity. Now help me live what I've learned. Please give me the courage to make financial decisions based on your values, not the world's values. Use my money to advance Your kingdom, reach lost souls, strengthen Your church, and bring glory to Your name. Help me finish my life as a faithful steward who invested in forever. In Jesus' name, Amen.*

. . .

"For where your treasure is, there your heart will be also." - Matthew 6:21

> **Your treasure reveals your heart. Your heart determines your legacy. Your legacy impacts eternity.**

Choose wisely, Invest in Eternity.

APPENDIX I: BIOGRAPHIES OF GREAT MEN OF FAITH

Charles Haddon Spurgeon (1834-1892)
The Prince of Preachers

Charles Spurgeon stands as one of the most powerful voices in history for the Gospel. Born in Essex, England, this remarkable man began preaching at the age of 16 and became the pastor of London's New Park Street Chapel at just 19. His congregation grew so large that they had to build the Metropolitan Tabernacle, which seated 6,000 people.

Spurgeon preached to over 10 million people during his lifetime, and his sermons were published every week for 25 years. He founded a college for pastors, an orphanage, and wrote over 140 books. Despite battling depression and physical ailments, Spurgeon never wavered in his commitment to Christ. His legacy continues to inspire preachers worldwide, proving that God uses broken vessels to accomplish great things.

Adoniram Judson (1788-1850)
Pioneer Missionary to Burma

Adoniram Judson's life demonstrates the cost and reward of radical obedience to Christ. Born in Massachusetts, Judson felt called to take the Gospel to foreign lands, a mission that few Americans had ever attempted. He and his wife Ann sailed to Burma (now Myanmar) in 1813, becoming America's first overseas missionaries.

Judson endured incredible hardships - imprisonment, torture, the death of his wife and children, and years of apparent failure. He spent six grueling years learning Burmese before seeing his first convert. Yet Judson persevered, translating the entire Bible into Burmese and establishing a church that grew to 7,000 members. His sacrifice opened the door for modern missions, showing that faithful endurance can transform nations.

William Carey (1761-1834)
Father of Modern Missions

William Carey transformed from a humble cobbler into the architect of the modern missionary movement. Born into poverty in England, Carey taught himself Latin, Greek, Hebrew, French, and Dutch while working as a shoemaker. His heart burned with passion to reach the unreached, famously declaring, "Expect great things from God; attempt great things for God."

Despite fierce opposition, Carey sailed to India in 1793. Over 41 years, he never took a furlough home. He mastered Sanskrit and

Bengali, translated the Bible into six languages, and founded Serampore College. Carey also fought against social evils like sati (widow burning) and the caste system. His life proves that God delights in using ordinary people with extraordinary faith to change the world.

William Wilberforce (1759-1833)
Champion of Human Freedom

William Wilberforce wielded political power to effect moral transformation, ultimately changing an empire. Born into wealth and privilege, this gifted orator entered Parliament at age 21. After his conversion to Christianity, Wilberforce felt called to use his influence for justice, declaring, "God has set before me two great objects: the abolition of the slave trade and the reformation of manners."

For 20 years, Wilberforce fought against the British slave trade, facing ridicule, death threats, and repeated defeats. His persistence paid off when Parliament finally abolished the slave trade in 1807. He continued fighting until slavery itself was outlawed throughout the British Empire in 1833, just days before his death. Wilberforce shows us that faithful Christians can be instruments of justice and mercy in the halls of power.

John Newton (1725-1807)
From Slave Trader to Grace Proclaimer

John Newton's story represents one of the most dramatic transformations in history. Born into a seafaring family, Newton became a slave trader, profiting from human misery and suffering. His life was marked by rebellion, cruelty, and spiritual darkness until God intervened through a violent storm at sea.

Newton's conversion didn't happen overnight, but when it took root, the change was revolutionary. He left the slave trade, studied for ministry, and became a pastor who devoted his life to proclaiming the grace that had saved "a wretch like me." Newton penned the beloved hymn "Amazing Grace" and used his influence to mentor young William Wilberforce in the fight against slavery.

Despite his past, Newton never forgot where grace had found him. He reportedly said, "I am not what I ought to be, I am not what I want to be, I am not what I hope to be in another world; but still I am not what I once used to be." His life proves that no one is beyond the reach of God's transforming grace.

George Whitefield (1714-1770)
The Great Awakening's Thunderous Voice

George Whitefield became one of the most powerful preachers of the 18th century, drawing crowds of thousands in an era without microphones or modern media. Born to a tavern keeper in

England, Whitefield discovered his calling while studying at Oxford, where he joined the "Holy Club" with John Wesley.

Whitefield's preaching sparked the Great Awakening in both America and Britain. He crossed the Atlantic 13 times, preaching to crowds that sometimes exceeded 20,000 people. Benjamin Franklin, though not a believer, marveled at Whitefield's ability to project his voice to such massive audiences. More importantly, his preaching led to countless conversions and transformed entire communities.

What set Whitefield apart was his willingness to sacrifice comfort for the sake of his calling. He gave away most of his income, lived a simple life, and endured persecution for the sake of the Gospel. His famous statement, "God had one Son without sin, but He has no sons without suffering," reflected his understanding that faithful service requires sacrifice. Through his ministry, churches were planted, believers were strengthened, and society was changed.

John Bunyan (1628-1688)
The Imprisoned Pilgrim

John Bunyan spent 12 years in Bedford jail for the "crime" of preaching without a license, but those prison walls became the birthplace of one of the most influential Christian allegories ever written. Born to a poor tinker's family, Bunyan struggled with deep spiritual anxiety before finding peace in Christ.

When authorities demanded that Bunyan stop preaching, he refused. "If you release me today, I will preach tomorrow," he declared. This commitment to truth over comfort cost him dearly - separation from his wife and children, loss of income, and years of confinement. Yet Bunyan used his imprisonment productively, writing "The Pilgrim's Progress" and other works that have influenced millions.

Bunyan's masterpiece narrates the journey of Christian from the City of Destruction to the Celestial City, illustrating the struggles and triumphs of a believer's life. His allegory has been translated into more languages than any other book except the Bible. Bunyan showed that faithfulness in small matters, such as refusing to compromise the truth, can produce extraordinary results that influence generations.

Jonathan Edwards (1703-1758)
America's Theological Giant

Jonathan Edwards combined brilliant intellect with passionate devotion to Christ, becoming colonial America's greatest theologian and a key figure in the Great Awakening. Born in Connecticut to a family of ministers, Edwards demonstrated exceptional intelligence from childhood, entering Yale at the age of 13.

Edwards is best known for his sermon "Sinners in the Hands of an Angry God," but his legacy extends far beyond one message. He served as pastor, theologian, philosopher, and eventually president of Princeton College. His careful study of Scripture and systematic theology helped shape American Christianity for generations.

What made Edwards remarkable was his ability to integrate rigorous scholarship with heartfelt piety. He made resolutions for holy living, including "Resolution One: I will live for God. Resolution Two: If no one else does, I still will." Edwards understood that true spiritual awakening required both sound doctrine and genuine conversion. His commitment to both theological precision and spiritual passion helped fuel the revival that transformed colonial America.

These men shared common traits: unwavering faith, persistent prayer, and a willingness to sacrifice comfort for the sake of their calling. They gave not just money, but their lives for the Gospel. Their lives remind us that God uses committed followers to accomplish His purposes in every generation. Each faced opposition, yet their legacies continue to inspire believers to live with courage and conviction.

ENDNOTES:

1 "Charles Spurgeon," Wikipedia; "Charles Haddon Spurgeon: A Brief Biography," Victorian Web

2 "Metropolitan Tabernacle: The 6000-seat Metropolitan Tabernacle at London, England," Granger Historical Picture Archive, 1890

3 "Charles H. Spurgeon: Did You Know?," Christianity Today, March 2, 2016

4 "Charles Spurgeon," Wikipedia; Victorian Web
5 "Did You Know That Charles Spurgeon Struggled with Depression?," Crossway, February 24, 2018; "Charles Spurgeon's Battle with Depression," The Gospel Coalition, May 19, 2022
6 "Adoniram Judson," Wikipedia
7 "Adoniram Judson," Wikipedia; Britannica
8 "Missionaries You Should Know: Adoniram Judson," IMB, February 21, 2025
9 "Adoniram Judson," Britannica
10 "Missionaries You Should Know: Adoniram Judson," IMB
11 "William Carey," Britannica; Wikipedia
12 "Expect Great Things From God Attempt Great Things for God," MARKINC.org, January 16, 2018
13 "William Carey," Wikipedia
14 "William Carey," Britannica
15 "William Carey," New World Encyclopedia; Wikipedia
16 "William Wilberforce," Wikipedia
17 "William Wilberforce," Britannica; Wikipedia
18 "William Wilberforce," Britannica
19 "William Wilberforce," Wikipedia
20 "John Newton," Wikipedia; "Amazing Grace," Wikipedia
21 "Amazing Grace," Wikipedia
22 "John Newton," Britannica; Christianity Today
23 "John Newton Quotes," Goodreads; "John Newton quote," AZquotes.com
24 "John Newton: From Slave Trader to Abolitionist Pastor," Religion & Liberty Online, October 19, 2023
25 "10 Interesting Facts about George Whitefield," FactsKing.com, January 31, 2020

26 "George Whitefield," Wikipedia
27 "George Whitefield," Wikipedia; Study.com
28 George Whitefield, Wealth https://reformedreader.org/rbs/whitefield/ mens.place.htm?
29 "John Bunyan," Wikipedia; Christian History Magazine
30 "John Bunyan," Wikipedia; Christian History Magazine
31 "The Pilgrim's Progress," Wikipedia; John Bunyan," Wikipedia
32 "The Pilgrim's Progress," Wikipedia
33 "Jonathan Edwards," Britannica; Wikipedia
34 "Jonathan Edwards," Britannica; Wikipedia
35 "Sinners in the Hands of an Angry God," Wikipedia; Crossway, July 8, 2018
36 "Jonathan Edwards," The Presidents of Princeton University; "Jonathan Edwards at the College of New Jersey," Princeton
37 "Jonathan Edwards," Britannica

APPENDIX II: QUOTES USED BY CHRISTIAN LEADERS

CHARLES SPURGEON (1834-1892)

"When you give to God's work, you are not giving to get, but giving because you've already gotten everything in Christ." - Day 1

"A man's treatment of money is the most decisive test of his character---how he makes it and how he spends it."
- Before We Begin

"Trials teach us what we are; they dig up the soil, and let us see what we are made of." - Day 4

"By perseverance, the snail reached the ark." - Day 5

"The best of men are men at best." - Day 7

"Every Christian is either a missionary or an impostor." - Day 10

"The Lord gets His best soldiers out of the highlands of affliction." - Day 12

"The Gospel is like a caged lion. It does not need to be defended, it just needs to be let out of its cage." - Day 13

"Giving is the thermometer of our love." - Day 15

"A church is not a gallery for the exhibition of eminent Christians, but a school for the education of imperfect ones." - Day 17

"A Bible that's falling apart usually belongs to someone who isn't." - Day 18

"It is not how much we have, but how much we enjoy, that makes happiness." - Day 20

"A good character is the best tombstone. Those who loved you and were helped by you will remember you when forget-me-nots have withered. Carve your name on hearts, not on marble." - Day 24

"The Bible was not given for our information but for our transformation." - Day 25

"A man wrapped up in himself makes a very small bundle." - Day 26

"I have learned to kiss the wave that throws me against the Rock of Ages." - Day 27

"I would rather be the means of saving one soul than of preaching to countless multitudes with no result." - Conclusion

WILLIAM CAREY (1761-1834)

"Prayer---secret, fervent, believing prayer---lies at the root of all personal godliness." - Day 2, Day 19

"I am not afraid of failure; I am afraid of succeeding at things that don't matter." - Day 5, Day 14

"Expect great things from God; attempt great things for God."
- Day 10, Appendix Biography

"To know the will of God, we need an open Bible and an open map."
- Day 12, Day 17

"I will go down, if you will hold the rope." - Day 18, Day 27

"The future is as bright as the promises of God." - Day 22

JOHN NEWTON (1725-1807)

"We serve a God who makes rough places smooth, and crooked things straight, but He does it in His time and in His way." - Day 5

"In times of affliction, we commonly meet with the sweetest experiences of the love of God." - Day 6

"How unspeakably wonderful to know that all our concerns are held in hands that bled for us." - Day 7

"If two angels were to receive at the same moment a commission from God, one to go down and rule earth's grandest empire, and the other to go and sweep the streets of its meanest village, it would be a matter of entire indifference to each which service fell to his lot." - Day 9

"I am not what I ought to be, I am not what I want to be, I am not what I hope to be in another world; but still I am not what I once used to be." - Day 12

"If I might trust my own heart, and if I might hope to stand in my strength, I might venture out; but since I know my weakness, I choose to stay by the fountain." - Day 13

"If I ever reach heaven, I expect to find three wonders there: first, to meet some I had not thought to see there; second, to miss some I had expected to see there; and third, the greatest wonder of all---to find myself there." - Day 17

"The Lord has led me about and instructed me and kept me as the apple of His eye." - Day 21

"Amazing grace, how sweet the sound, that saved a wretch like me." - Day 23

"My memory is nearly gone, but I remember two things: That I am a great sinner, and that Christ is a great Savior." - Day 27

"John Newton, clerk, once an infidel and libertine, a servant of slaves in Africa, was, by the rich mercy of our Lord and Savior Jesus Christ, preserved, restored, pardoned, and appointed to preach the faith he had long labored to destroy." - Conclusion (Gravestone)

ADONIRAM JUDSON (1788-1850)

"There is no success without sacrifice. If you succeed without sacrifice, it is because someone has suffered before you. If you sacrifice without success, it is because someone will succeed after you." - Day 11

"The motto of every missionary, whether preacher, printer, or schoolmaster, ought to be 'Devoted for Life.'" - Day 17

"The prospects are as bright as the promises of God." - Day 20

"I never was deeply interested in any object, I never prayed sincerely and earnestly for anything, but it came at some time." - Day 27

"A life once spent is irrevocable. It will remain to be contemplated through eternity." - Day 28

GEORGE WHITEFIELD (1714-1770)

"*We are immortal until our work on earth is done.*" - Day 3, Day 22

"*God had one Son without sin, but He has no sons without suffering.*" - Day 8

JOHN BUNYAN (1628-1688)

"*You have not lived today until you have done something for someone who can never repay you.*" - Day 4, Day 19

"*I have never lived so cheerfully as I do now...the love of Christ constrains me.*" - Day 11

"*The church is the pillar and ground of the truth.*" - Day 14

"*The enemy so assaulted me with doubts and fears concerning my eternal state, that because of my terror I could not tell what to do.*" - Day 22

"*If you release me today, I will preach tomorrow.*" - Appendix Biography

JONATHAN EDWARDS (1703-1758)

"*Resolution One: I will live for God. Resolution Two: If no one else does, I will.*" - Day 3, Appendix Biography

"The happiness of the creature consists in rejoicing in God, by which also God is magnified and exalted." - Referenced in planning

Dear Investor,

As we reach the end of our journey together through these pages, I want to leave you with a truth that can transform not just your life, but the lives of countless others around the world: **Your generosity has the power to change everything.**

The local church remains God's chosen instrument for advancing His kingdom on earth. When you give through your local church, you're not just supporting programs or buildings—you're investing in eternal transformation. You're funding the rescue of the lost, the healing of the broken, and the hope of the hopeless. Every dollar becomes a seed planted in the fertile soil of God's purposes.

Your church is your front line for kingdom impact. It's where your heart connects with God's heart for your community and beyond. When you give with faith and intention, you become a partner in the greatest mission ever conceived—bringing the love of Christ to a world that needs it.

If You Don't Have a Church Home

If you find yourself without a local church family, I want you to know something: **I would love to be your pastor.** This isn't just words on a page—this is a genuine invitation from my heart to yours. You were created for community, designed for purpose, and destined for impact.

At City United Church, we believe every person matters to God, and that includes you. We're not just another church; we're a global family united by one mission: to see lives transformed by the radical love of Jesus Christ.

Join Our Global Family

City United Church is reaching people around the world because we believe the Gospel knows no boundaries. We are an authentic community where masks come off and real life happens. We practice transparency because pretense never produced spiritual growth. We pursue transformation because that's why Jesus came —to make all things new.

Our family continues to witness the power of generous hearts transforming lives. When our people give, miracles happen. Communities change, families heal, hope rises from ashes, lives that once seemed beyond repair become testimonies of God's incredible grace.

Take Your Next Step

I invite you to discover more about our family at City United Church. Discover our heart, mission, and vision for transformation. Discover how God is at work in our community and how you can be part of something greater than yourself.

Download our app on all platforms and begin your spiritual growth journey with us. Access teachings that will strengthen your faith, connect with others who share your values, and find resources that will help you grow in your relationship with God. This app isn't just technology—it's your gateway to transformation.

A Personal Request

As we continue to plant missional communities and change lives around the world, I ask for your prayers. Pray for wisdom as we lead. Pray for resources as we expand. Pray for hearts to be opened as we share the gospel. Pray for protection as we advance against darkness in New England.

But more than your prayers, I invite you to consider being part of our family. Whether through your presence, your service, or your generous giving, you can join us in this incredible mission of transformation.

The Kingdom of God advances through ordinary people who say "yes" to extraordinary purposes. You are one prayer, one step, one decision away from joining the most significant movement in human history.

The question isn't whether God can use you—He absolutely can and wants to. The question is: **Will you let Him?**

Your Kingdom impact starts now.

The best is yet to come because God Is Bigger!

Visit us at CityUnited.church or download our app to begin your spiritual growth journey today. We can't wait to welcome you into our family. www.cityunited.church

| THE CHURCH VITALITY NETWORK.COM

The Church Vitality Network (CVN) is a resource for churches seeking revitalization and renewal. It offers a variety of resources, including assessments, coaching, consulting, cohorts, and classes, designed to help churches improve their health. CVN emphasizes personalized plans, creativity, and encouragement to help churches navigate their unique paths to renewal.

DR. GARY MORITZ is married to Dr. Jana Moritz, and they serve as a ministry team, working side by side in the local church and within church-planting and missions organizations. They have two grown daughters and a son-in-law, who lead and serve in the local church. He is the lead pastor of City United Church in Lunenburg, MA.

Gary works for Liberty University as a *Subject Matter Expert* in Church Revitalization and as an assistant professor in the online School of Divinity. He also serves as the Director of Church Revitalization for the Baptist Churches of New England, whose focus is on providing an established network of support for pastors and churches in New England enabling them to thrive.

Gary established The Church Vitality Network, an online platform that connects churches with resources for health in pastoring, revitalization, and renewal through a digital hub.

Made in the USA
Middletown, DE
01 October 2025

18210885R00124